D1155893

Robert Duncan

Twayne's United States Authors Series

Warren French, Editor

University College of Swansea, Wales

TUSAS 526

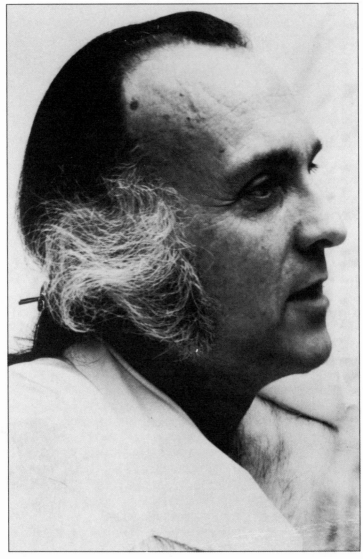

ROBERT DUNCAN
(1919–   )
Photograph by Matthew Foley reproduced
courtesy of New Directions Publishing Corp.

Robert Duncan

By Mark Andrew Johnson

Central Missouri State University

Twayne Publishers
A Division of G.K. Hall & Co. • *Boston*

811
D91 ʒʒ̇

Robert Duncan
Mark Andrew Johnson

Copyright 1988 by G.K. Hall & Co.
All rights reserved.
Published by Twayne Publishers
A Division of G.K. Hall & Co.
70 Lincoln Street
Boston, Massachusetts 02111

Copyediting supervised by Lewis DeSimone
Book production by Janet Zietowski
Book design by Barbara Anderson

Typeset in 11 pt. Garamond
by Compset, Inc. of Beverly, Massachusetts

Printed on permanent/durable acid-free paper
and bound in the United States of America

Library of Congress Cataloging in Publication Data

Johnson, Mark, 1948–
    Robert Duncan.

    (Twayne's United States authors series ; TUSAS 526)
    Bibliography: p.
    Includes index.
    1. Duncan, Robert Edward, 1919–   —Criticism and
interpretation.   I. Title.   II. Series.
PS3507.U629Z73   1988   811'.54   87-17738
ISBN 0-8057-7511-0 (alk. paper)

For Mary Kay

UNIVERSITY LIBRARIES
CARNEGIE-MELLON UNIVERSITY
PITTSBURGH, PENNSYLVANIA 15213

Contents

About the Author

Mark A. Johnson was born in Erie, Pennsylvania in 1948. He received his B.A. from Gannon College in 1970, and his M.A. and Ph.D. from Ohio University in 1973 and 1977. He is an associate professor of English at Central Missouri State University in Warrensburg, Missouri. His essays and reviews have appeared in *Sagetrieb, Ironwood, Contemporary Poetry,* the *Southern Literary Journal,* the *Journal of Modern Literature,* and elsewhere. He edited a collection of essays, *Modern American Cultural Criticism* (1983), and has received two National Endowment for the Humanities summer seminar grants. He and his wife, Mary Kay, have two sons, Eric and Matthew.

Preface

Robert Duncan does not need this book. While he has been generous in his support and correspondence, he has always refused to engage in marketplace concerns. Repulsed by the commercialism, hype, and trivia, he has insisted on the primacy of the author's concerns over those of the printer or publisher, frequently at the expense of his "career" and reputation.

Further, both he and I would insist that this book be secondary to the poetry itself. Duncan makes large demands on his readers: as he wrote to William Everson in 1940, "I would bring a gift of unrest among men."[1] No single book could encompass Duncan's large and complex achievement, and this one should be read merely as an introduction. Even so, coverage of his biography and of the all-important context of his contemporaries has been sharply limited here out of necessity. Duncan's work is unfashionably eclectic and allusive, so that even well-intentioned readers can be put off, at first, by its difficulty. To look at the issue more positively, however, questions of meaning have always been the main source of poetry's and criticism's interest for the nonspecialist—the "hidden meaning" that so obsesses the naive but good-willed student. Let this book serve as a helpful entry to both content and form, a modest response to Duncan's admonition of critics' ignoring, or ignorance, of content at the expense of structure or language. But this book must not be used to replace Duncan's large demands on his readers. As he described it at the recent Ezra Pound conference at San Jose State University, poetry is a process of self-education, for each poet and reader.

Duncan's work is inexhaustibly rich, and sometimes inescapably frustrating. But our assignment is not perfection, but, etymologically, *perficere*: to carry on an ever unfolding, never completed reading. Duncan's poetry exemplifies his own statement that "the poetry that most moved us moved us to a need for poetry" (*Caesar's Gate*, xl).

I am happy to acknowledge the assistance of a number of people, without whose help this book would not exist. They are, of course, not responsible for its shortcomings. As the thought is prior to the form, Robert DeMott stands behind my work as a mentor and model of what I aspire to be as a scholar and a teacher. Robert Duncan has been a generous correspondent, and I appreciate his support for what he must regard as a dubious project. My editors at Twayne, Warren French and Athenaide Dallett, encouraged my labors and improved their results. Two primary Duncan scholars, Robert Bertholf and Michael Davidson, have been most helpful with information and suggestions. Their staffs, at the Poetry Collection at SUNY at Buffalo and the Archive for New Poetry at the University of California at San Diego, respectively, were most professional and fully cooperative during my visits. At a germinal stage of my interest in Duncan, an NEH summer seminar with Roy Harvey Pearce provided crucial nurture; another one, with Giles Gunn, helped develop my thought; and later, an NEH travel-to-libraries grant aided my research in Buffalo. My colleague Gail Crump forced me to strengthen my arguments with his friendly contentiousness. Ann Wilson Fisher, Noreen Brown, and Kim Schaefer deserve more thanks than words can express for their work translating my manuscript to type. Finally, my wife, Mary Kay, and my sons, Eric and Matthew, have made large personal sacrifices while I wrote this book. Having such people to share this with makes it worthwhile.

Mark Andrew Johnson

Central Missouri State University

Abbreviations

Because so much of Duncan's work is cited here, in order to avoid distracting notes the following abbreviations are used in the text. For full bibliographic data, see the bibliography at the end of the book. "The H.D. Book" is cited by part, chapter, and page; thus, "HD 2.7.60" is part 2, chapter 7, page 60. Interviews are cited by the last names of the interviewers.

BB	*Bending the Bow*
CG	*Caesar's Gate*
D	*Derivations*
FC	*Fictive Certainties*
FD	*The First Decade*
GW	*Ground Work: Before the War*
OF	*The Opening of the Field*
"Reading Zukofsky"	"As Testimony: Reading Zukofsky These Forty Years"
RB	*Roots and Branches*
YAC	*The Years as Catches*

Acknowledgments

Grateful acknowledgment is made for permission to quote from the writings of Robert Duncan from the following sources:

From the audio tapes in the Archive for New Poetry, Mandeville Department of Special Collections, Central University Library, University of California, San Diego, quoted by permission of Robert Duncan.

From Robert Duncan, *Medieval Scenes 1950 and 1959,* quoted by permission of Robert Duncan, Robert Bertholf, and the Friends of the Kent State University Libraries.

From letters from Robert Duncan to Jonathan Williams, Poetry/Rare Book Collection, State University of New York, Buffalo, New York, quoted by permission of Robert J. Bertholf, curator.

From Robert Duncan, *The First Decade,* copyright © 1968 and Robert Duncan, *Derivations,* copyright © 1968, quoted by permission of Robert Duncan.

Reprinted by permission of New Directions Publishing Corporation and Robert Duncan:

Robert Duncan, *Ground Work.* Copyright © 1968, 1969, 1970, 1971, 1972, 1975, 1976, 1977, 1982, 1984 by Robert Duncan.

Robert Duncan, *Fictive Certainties.* Copyright © 1955, 1956, 1961, 1965, 1966, 1968, 1978, 1983, 1985 by Robert Duncan.

Robert Duncan, *The Opening of the Field.* Copyright © 1960 by Robert Duncan.

Robert Duncan, *Roots and Branches.* Copyright © 1964 by Robert Duncan.

Robert Duncan, *Bending the Bow.* Copyright © 1963, 1964, 1965, 1966, 1967, 1968 by Robert Duncan. "In the Place of a Passage," "Benefice Passage," "The Light Passage," and "Eye of God Passage" were first published in *Poetry.*

Portions of this book appeared earlier as "Robert Duncan's 'Momentous Inconclusions,'" *Sagetrieb* 2 (Summer/Fall 1983); "'Passages': Cross-sections of the Universe," *Ironwood 22,* 11, no. 2 (Fall 1983), a special Robert Duncan issue; and "'An Inheritance of Spirit': Robert Duncan and Walt Whitman," coauthored with Robert DeMott, in *Robert Duncan: Scales of the Marvelous,* ed. Robert J. Bertholf and Ian W. Reid (New York: New Directions, 1979). I thank the editors for permission to reprint.

Chronology

1919 Born Edward Howard Duncan, in Oakland, California, 7 January to Edward Howard and Marguerite Wesley Duncan. When his mother dies shortly after his birth, Duncan is adopted and raised as Robert Edward Symmes.

1922 Injuring an eye in a fall, Duncan becomes cross-eyed.

1935 Death of stepfather.

1936–1938 Attends the University of California at Berkeley. Circle includes Virginia Admiral, Mary and Lilli Fabilli, and Pauline Kael. Publishes first poems in the school literary magazine, the *Occident*.

1939–1945 Lives in the East. In New York City, part of Anaïs Nin's circle; lives for a time with Sanders Russell and Jack Johnson in Woodstock.

1939 Edits *Ritual* (in 1940, the *Experimental Review*) with Virginia Admiral.

1941 Psychiatric discharge from the army.

1942 Resumes original surname. Meets Kenneth Rexroth.

1943 Marries Marjorie McKee. After her abortion a few months later, they divorce.

1944 Publishes "The Homosexual in Society" in *Politics*.

1946 Returns to Berkeley, studying medieval and Renaissance civilization under Ernst Kantorowicz. Fellow students include Jack Spicer and Robin Blaser.

1947 *Heavenly City, Earthly City*. Visits Ezra Pound at St. Elizabeth's Hospital. Meets Charles Olson in Berkeley.

1949 *Poems, 1948–49*.

1950 *Medieval Scenes*.

1951 Begins his continuing relationship with artist Jess Collins.

1952   Begins publishing work in *Origin* and the *Black Mountain Review*.

1955–1956   Visits Robert Creeley in Mallorca.

1955   *Caesar's Gate: Poems 1949–50.*

1956   Teaches at Black Mountain College, April–August.

1956–1957   Assistant Director of the Poetry Center at San Francisco State, September to June.

1957   Participates in Jack Spicer's "Poetry as Magic" workshop. Charles Olson lectures on A. N. Whitehead at Duncan and Jess's house. Union League Civic and Arts Foundation Prize (*Poetry* magazine).

1958   *Letters: Poems MCMLIII–MCMLVI.*

1959   *Faust Foutu.*

1960   *The Opening of the Field.*

1961   Harriet Monroe Memorial Prize (*Poetry* magazine).

1963   Guggenheim Fellowship.

1964   *Roots and Branches. Writing Writing: Stein Imitations.* Levinson Prize (*Poetry* magazine).

1965   *Medea at Kolchis: The Maiden Head. The Sweetness and Greatness of Dante's Divine Comedy.*

1966–1967   National Endowment for the Arts Grants.

1966   *The Years as Catches: First Poems, 1939–46.*

1967   *Audit/Poetry* 4, no. 3 features Duncan.

1968   *Bending the Bow. The Truth & Life of Myth.*

1969   *The First Decade: Selected Poems, 1940–1950. Derivations: Selected Poems, 1950–56.*

1970   *Tribunals: Passages 31–35.*

1974   *Maps* 6, a special Duncan issue.

1980   National Endowment for the Arts Fellowship.

1983   *Ironwood* 22, a special Duncan issue.

1984   *Ground Work, Volume I: Before the War.* Fred Cody Award for literary excellence and community involvement (Bay Area Book Review Association).

1985   National Poetry Award. *Sagetrieb* 4, no. 2/3, a special Duncan issue.

Chapter One

Biography

Robert Duncan was born Edward Howard Duncan in Oakland, California, on 7 January 1919, to Edward Howard and Marguerite Wesley Duncan. Either from the childbirth or from the flu epidemic of that year, his mother died almost immediately after his birth, and his father, a day laborer, was forced to put him up for adoption. His foster parents, "orthodox theosophists," chose him on the basis of his astrological configuration. Duncan grew up as Robert Edward Symmes and published some two dozen poems under that name before resuming his original surname in 1942.

His family's hermetic lore and the fables and nursery rhymes of his childhood are a major influence in his work. "I have consciously proposed that I would keep alive and at work as primaries earliest experiences and structures," he says in "The Self in Postmodern Poetry." "I would not reprove the child in me in my also being adolescent, in my also being grown-up. Hence I seek out and fortify even embarrassing sentiments—sentimentalities they can be seen to be by those critics who have put away childish things" (FC 220). Growing up in the "closed community" of Bakersfield, the young man saw that "there would be a place for me, if I completed my professional training [as an architect] and took up my father's office, if I came to the right conclusions . . . But something in me did not want to come to such conclusions" (FC 113). Instead, he was drawn to the world of his grandmother, his Aunt Fay, and his parents, "this despised way" of the occult and the fabulous. He remembers waiting in an anteroom as a boy: "My eyes have seen the veil, the double or triple moving depths of bead curtain, that in my work may still be my fascination with the movement of meaning beyond or behind meaning, of shifting vowels and consonants—beads of sound, of separate strands that convey the feeling of one weave. . . . There is something about looking behind things. There is the fact that I am not an occultist or a mystic but a poet, a maker-up of things" (HD 2.2.37–38).

The actual lore is less important to Duncan than the predisposition to belief in the fabulous. As he told Abbott and Shurin, "We have

1

something we are meant to do in our lives and we have also something
that is to be revealed to us; so the life is both the text we write in
living and is also a text we read which is written for us and we constantly read" (*Sunshine* 6). He was particularly influenced by the
grown-ups' comparing America to Atlantis, which "had found some
key to the universe and had unlocked forbidden, destroying powers."
Told he belonged to another Atlantean generation "that would see once
more last things and the destruction of a world," the boy had a recurring "Atlantis dream," which confirmed his belief that "I had a part in
the fabulous." The dream's motifs—of a hill, a field that seemed alive,
a circle of children dancing in the field, an underground cavern, a stone
chair, a flood—recur in much of Duncan's poetry, most notably in *The
Opening of the Field*. For Duncan, such dreams are not willed but compel: "There is a sense in which the 'poet' of a poem forces us as writer
or reader to obey a compelling form, the necessities of the poem, so
that the poet has a likeness to the dreamer of the dream and to the
creator of our living reality; dream, reality, and the poem, seem to be
one" (HD 1.5.16–18). The importance to Duncan's work of fairy tales,
dreams, and hermetic lore cannot be overemphasized, for he has indeed
kept them alive "as primaries."

In 1922, he injured one eye in a fall and became cross-eyed. Since
his very way of seeing blurs distinctions and identities, he tells us,
"I had the double reminder always, the vertical and horizontal displace-
ment in vision that later became separated, specialized into a near and
a far sight. One image to the right and above the other. Reach out and
touch. Point to the one that is really there" (RB 14). Here and in such
poems as "A Poem Slow Beginning" and "Crosses of Harmony and
Disharmony" he explores such vision, which he relates to Alfred North
Whitehead's concept of "presentational immediacy."

After receiving some very important encouragement from Edna
Keough, a high school teacher, Duncan attended the University of
California at Berkeley from 1936 to 1938, publishing his first poems
in the school's literary magazine, the *Occident,* and joining a circle of
friends that included Mary and Lilli Fabilli, Virginia Admiral, and
Pauline Kael. "By my eighteenth year," as he says in the introduction
to *The Years as Catches,* "I recognized in poetry my sole and ruling
vocation." His homosexuality also surfaced at this time, and he left
Berkeley to accompany his lover to the East Coast. Duncan directly
addresses the significance of his homosexuality to his art: "Perhaps the
sexual irregularity underlay and led to the poetic; neither as homosex-

ual nor as poet could one take over readily the accepted paradigms and conventions of the Protestant ethic" (YAC i–ii).

For several years he lived in the East, associating with the circle of Anaïs Nin in New York City (including at times Henry Miller, Lawrence Durrell, George Barker, Nicolas Calas, and others) and with a group of poets in Woodstock that included Sanders Russell and Jack Johnson. Receiving a psychiatric discharge from the army in 1941, he continued publishing poems, and with Virginia Admiral and Russell edited *Ritual* (later the *Experimental Review*).

During a brief return to the West Coast in 1942 he lived with Hamilton and Mary Tyler[1] and met Kenneth Rexroth, the influential figure for many of the young poets of the San Francisco Renaissance a few years later. Rexroth introduced him to the poetry of H. D. and Edith Sitwell at this time.

Returning to New York, in the spring of 1943 Duncan married Marjorie McKee, at a time when their relationship was already deteriorating. His story, "Love," indicates the marriage was doomed from the start. After her abortion a few months later, they divorced. By the spring of 1944, Duncan had left New York for a few months in Florida, a dark period that extended to his subsequent period in New York. He was sexually adrift and refers to himself as a gigolo (Abbott and Shurin, *Sunshine* 5).

In 1944, he published his essay "The Homosexual in Society," in *Politics*.[2] The essay was courageous, not only because it was the first such essay, signed and acknowledged by one "willing to take in his own persecution a battlefront toward human freedom" as Jews and blacks has done in their struggles; and not only because its author paid a very real price, immediately and over the years, for his public position; but also because it attacked as well the cult of homosexual superiority as itself "an incredible force of exclusion and blindness" (210). Indeed, if anything his attack on such "witchdoctors in the modern chaos" was far harsher than his criticism of the inhumanity of the larger society, for they had twisted the achievement of Proust, Melville, and especially Hart Crane, whose suffering, rebellion, and love "are sources of poetry for him not because they are what make him different from, superior to, mankind, but because he saw in them his link with mankind; he saw in them his sharing in universal human experience" (210).

One immediate result of the essay was John Crowe Ransom's refusal to print in the *Kenyon Review* "An African Elegy," which had already been accepted before the essay appeared. Duncan now refers to the

episode as an escape: "So I was *out,* just read out, out, out, at a point
when I would have been *in* at the wrong place." With characteristic
humor, he observes that the issue, which included W. H. Auden, Paul
Goodman, and Parker Tyler, looked like "a coffee klatsch. I'm glad I
wasn't in there; I would have been read not as an advertisement but as
a conformist" (Cohn and O'Donnell 524).

In the fall of 1945 he returned to California, living again with the
Tylers, this time on a farm at Treesbank, and entering into the political
and literary circles of San Francisco. The following year he returned to
Berkeley, studying medieval and Renaissance culture under the great
scholar Ernst Kantorowicz. He had written *Medieval Scenes* before this
period of formal study, and *The Venice Poem* was soon to follow. Long
before Allen Ginsberg's *Howl* focused national attention on San Francisco, a "renaissance" had begun in the lives and works of Duncan and
Philip Whalen, Jack Spicer, Robin Blaser, and Philip Lamantia. An
account of the personal and poetic friendships, rivalries, and jealousies
of this period would require a book in itself (one such as Lewis Elling-
ham's *The Spicer Circle,* which has begun to appear in small magazines).
Duncan's relationship with Spicer was particularly stormy, and he has
often expressed his regret for his own behavior in some of their feuds.
At the same time, he has also testified to Spicer's importance to his
own work as "an original of such power in my own imagination as a
poet that whole areas of my creative consciousness still seem to me to
have to do with a matter that was ultimately from him."[3]

In the summer of 1947 Duncan traveled to Washington, D.C., to
spend two days with Ezra Pound at St. Elizabeth's Hospital. Fully
cognizant of their irreconcilable political beliefs, Duncan still acknowledged Pound as an important poetic influence. Upon his return West
he met Charles Olson, the anthropologist and poet who would also
exercise a profound influence on Duncan's work. This first meeting,
however, was uneventful, since Olson was then known primarily as an
archeologist and Melville scholar.

In 1950 Duncan met the painter Jess Collins (who prefers to be
called Jess) and on New Year's Day, 1951, the two established a household. This continuing relationship has brought a stability to Duncan's
life, and the two have influenced each other's work. "A student of
abstract expressionists such as Clifford Still, Edward Corbett, and Has-
sell Smith at the San Francisco Art Institute," according to Michael
Davidson, "Jess has been associated with a group of artists including
Harry Jacobus, Lili Fenichel and Brock Brockway. His love for the

romantic tradition in art and literature brought Jess's concerns close to Duncan's. Much of the poet's concern with the collagist's art is drawn from Jess's monumental paste-ups and collages."[4] The influence of Jess's work on Duncan's is evident in Duncan's description of it in "Iconographical Extensions," an essay that accompanies *Translations by Jess:* "The painter works not to conclude the elements of the painting but to set them into motion, not to bind the colors but to free them, to release the force of their interrelationships" (iv). As Duncan points out near the end of the essay, "writing here of his work I find myself coming into realizations of elements of my own poetics that have been born in contemplations of paintings and paste-ups" (xiii). The continuing importance of art, especially contemporary art, for Duncan's work is further manifested in his essays on George Herms and Wallace Berman.

Duncan and Jess were active in another group of poets, "The Maidens," who used to gather for readings and plays in the mid-1950s. Sometimes deliberately childish, this group also included the poet and filmmaker James Broughton, Eve Triem, Madeline Gleason, and Helen Adam.

In the pages of Cid Corman's *Origin,* a new constellation of poets also began to appear, later to be known as the Black Mountain group, after the short-lived but influential college in North Carolina: Charles Olson, Robert Creeley, Duncan, of course, and later Denise Levertov, Paul Blackburn, and Larry Eigner. Ed Dorn and John Weiners were students at the college, where as rector Olson gathered a faculty that included himself, Duncan, John Cage, and many others.

After teaching at Black Mountain from April to August of 1956, Duncan helped to found and served as assistant director of the Poetry Center at San Francisco State from September 1956 to June 1957. In the spring of 1957 he participated, with some frustrations, in Jack Spicer's "Poetry as Magic" workshop. The passionate feeling for poetry of all these groups can be seen in Duncan's chapbook, *As Testimony,* which grew out of an argument about poetry, at "one of a series of meetings of poets," this one on 23 February 1958. Of the argument, Duncan says, "We were moved perhaps rightly to break then the damnd social benevolence and to rage even stupidly against the indifference that protected our private individual emotions. For Poetry depends everywhere upon the old sympathetic heart, upon 'little passionate currents, often conflicting,' and cannot keep the peace" (17).

By the late fifties Duncan had completed *Letters* and had begun
working on the first book of his major phase, *The Opening of the Field*.
Charles Olson's essay "Projective Verse" and his 1957 lectures on
Whitehead at Duncan and Jess's Potrero Hill home in San Francisco
were both important to Duncan at this time, though he often chose to
play the heretic to Olson's position, just as he often had previously to
Spicer's. His "The Artist's View" statements prompted Olson's sharp
response, "Against Wisdom as Such,"[5] which to this day Duncan regards not as an attack but as a helpful lever on his own position (see
Cohn and O'Donnell 515–17; Mesch 95). Since Olson's death in 1970,
Duncan says, "I feel I'm not a part of 'current literature' . . . not with
an antagonism to history, but with a much more deliberate sense of
what's really going on" (Cohn and O'Donnell 515).

After three active decades, which culminated in the three major
books of poetry in the 1960s—*The Opening of the Field, Roots and
Branches,* and *Bending the Bow*—Duncan announced in 1972 that he
would not publish another major collection until 1983. *Ground Work,
Volume One: Before the War* appeared in 1984, with *Volume Two: In the
Dark* announced for 1989. In his maturity, even as he garners more
recognition and honors, Duncan has self-consciously withdrawn from
the public role, which demands regular book publication to keep one's
name before the reviewers and readers. In attending not to personal
reputation, not to movements and fashions, but rather to that "more
deliberate sense of what's really going on," Duncan has taken a larger
hand in the printing and distribution of his work, at the expense of its
commercial success. More important, he has directly addressed the creative crisis of the contemporary artist. "I saw my own personal life
belonging to a larger human life that was foreign to the society into
which I had been born, to the American way, to the capitalist ethic
with its identification of work with earning a wage and of the work
with a saleable commodity, and with its ruthless exploitation of human
energies for profit" (YAC vii). That creative crisis is a crisis of content
as well as of form, a confrontation between idealism and "what we call
the Real, the pervading triumph of mercantile utilitarianism" which
is supported by "the economy of wage-slavery and armed forces, and
over all, the threat of impending collapse or disastrous war. We too,
in a hostile environment, taking our faith and our home in our exile,
live in creative crisis" (HD 1.6.52–53).

Comparing our drive toward self-destruction with Oedipus' need "to
make his blindness actual," Duncan confronts men with "the strange

refusal to see what they are doing or to hear what they are saying just when they are most engaged in their own self-destruction" (58–59). Grounded in the faith that "we can know or imagine no more about the good of the poem than we know or imagine about the good of the society" (HD Day Book 41), these are a life and a poetry that matter.

Chapter Two
Derivations

"I am a derivative poet," Duncan has declared, embracing a critically pejorative term with a full awareness of his tradition, of his origins. His constellation of masters ranges from the pre-Socratics to Olson and Zukofsky, and his allusions include fairy tales and theories of modern physics. "My vision of poetry," he has stated, "has been drawn from Carlyle as well as from Whitman, from Dante, from Burckhardt, from Pater and Symonds as well as from Pound or Olson—wherever another man's vision leads my spirit towards a larger feeling" (HD 2.7.60–61).

The reader of any poem must first confront the text, including its allusions without subordinating the poem to its annotations. Duncan's readers need not scurry out to read everything that he has read, since such a feat is no more practical than trying to duplicate his life experience. The purpose of this chapter, therefore, is simply to trace what Duncan calls "an inheritance of spirit." Without at least some awareness of Duncan's major influences among predecessors and contemporaries, the reader loses an essential sense of the poetry's context and method, indeed of Duncan's poetics itself.[1]

First, Duncan is careful to distinguish between his concern with origins and an inflated valuing of originality. H. D. and D. H. Lawrence, he tells us, "sought not originality but to recover a commune of spirit in the image." Just as Hermes guided poets in the past and as Virgil guided Dante, "briefly, in the Cantos, Plotinus appears to rescue Pound from the hell-mire of politicians and dead issues." Because he is unwilling to follow the inspiration of his own poem, however, "it is the originality of Pound that mars his intelligence. The goods of the intellect are communal; there is a *virtu* or power that flows from the language itself, a fountain of man's meanings, and the poet seeking the help of this source awakens first to the guidance of those who have gone before in the art, then the guidance of the meanings and dreams that all who have ever stored the honey of the invisible in the hive have prepared" (HD 2.10.60, 64).

In this ongoing participation in "a community of meanings" in which "the old roots will stir again" (HD 2.2.17), Duncan moves in the spirit of such predecessors as Carlyle, Emerson, and George MacDonald, cognizant of what Shelley called the one great poem that all poets are writing. Because Duncan's tradition is not only wide-ranging but heterodox, however, he has been charged with a willful obscurantism and pretentiousness by some critics. Setting aside the preposterous critical situation that reprimands a poet for being learned or for expecting his reader to put forth some effort, one still must admit that Duncan's poetry can be difficult and even frustrating in its allusiveness. Acknowledging in an interview that he takes for granted knowledge of Dante, Milton, and Pound, Duncan argues that doing so engages and even alters the work of those poets, recalling Eliot's "Tradition and the Individual Talent." His basic argument here is that he wants his reader to be involved with his primary experience, which includes in his "conglomerate" not only Milton and Dante but also the novels of Charles Williams, Pindar's poetry, and even Krazy Kat. The attempt to engage as many minds as possible in a living, active tradition is a practice that should be encouraged rather than disparaged. Keeping in mind Duncan's distinction between the arrogance or foolishness of thinking one has "knowledge of the whole" as opposed to the importance of "acknowledging" that whole, we have the basics of Duncan's definition of the Romantic tradition as "the intellectual adventure of not knowing" (FC 46). The best answer to the charge of obscurantism—in this poet's work and that of many other modern poets—lies, then, in the recognition of the challenge or invitation to participate to the best of one's ability in the whole life of mankind's culture.

Just why Duncan includes particular authors in his chrestomathy and not others is much more than a matter of taste. His imaginative synthesis is grounded in what he calls "a felt need," an intuitive recognition of "the real" in others' work: "I can have no recourse to taste. The work of Denise Levertov or Robert Creeley or Larry Eigner belongs not to my appreciations but to my immediate concerns in living. That I might 'like' or 'dislike' a poem of Zukofsky's or Charles Olson's means nothing where I turn to their work as evidence of the real. . . . Taste can be imposed, but love and knowledge are conditions that life imposes upon us" (FC 104).

All this is not to say that Duncan's derivations are all for the good. In addition to frustrating some readers and consequently reducing the size of his audience, Duncan's use of sources has at times overwhelmed his own voice. His early poetry especially suffered, to the point that for some time he refused to acknowledge his own poem *Heavenly City, Earthly City*. His *Writing Writing: Stein Imitations*, written in the early 1950s and published in 1964, is a book of finger exercises of which he has said, "I sat down and for a year imitated Gertrude Stein. Tried to trick myself entirely. . . . A fake Cezanne painted by Duncan is an authentic Duncan—and a fake. Duncan painted by Duncan is a lovely proposition. So then I came off it" (*Reflector* 53). Nonetheless, he continues to acknowledge such work as a necessary element in the collage of his poetic achievement.

While a book, much less a single chapter, could not hope to deal with the full encyclopedic range of Duncan's sources, five particular areas of focus do present themselves: the occult, from fairy tales to the Zohar; Whitman and other Romantic writers; Dante; philosophers and linguists; and Duncan's contemporaries.

The Occult

Duncan has publicly lamented the "demythologized education" of many young poets he meets: "The separation of Church and State has been interpreted to mean that the lore of God is the matter of the private individual, and the myths of the Old and New Testament are no longer part of our common learning." One young poet studying Duncan's Pindar poem called the story of Eros and Psyche a mere fairy tale from Apuleis; for Duncan it is both a bedtime story *and* "the fable embodying the doctrine of the soul" (FC 18). A recurring theme of this study is Duncan's insistent interrogation of limits and boundaries. This particular area of interest—mystery, enchantment, God, childlike faith and enthusiasm—is only one more area in which this poet refuses to accept the boundaries of common sense and convention. In so doing, he has been charged with sentimentality, if anything a more devastating critical taboo than obscurity, and he has met that charge directly: "I have consciously proposed that I would keep alive and at work as primaries earliest experiences and structures. I would not reprove the child in me in my also being adolescent, in my also being grown-up. Hence I seek out and fortify even embarrassing sentiments—sentimentalities they can be seen to be by those critics who have put away childish things" (FC 220). The direct rebuke to such critics and to other Pauline limitations invokes the direct gain his border crossing incurs, an active role for poetry in "the very primordial pattern from which the life of the soul flows" (FC 18).

Consequently, Duncan takes no pains to conceal his embrace of fairy tales, recalling his introduction to Celtic myths under Edna Keough, the teacher who inspired him "with Stephen's *Crock of Gold* and *Deirdre,* with books of *Fionn* and the old world of glamors and wishes. 'Escape literature' such is called by those who would be wardens of the prison of their particular realities" (HD 1.2.30).

Duncan likens the "trips" of the shaman, medium, poet, dreamer, and child, noting that "the fairy tale is the immortal residue of the spirit that seeks to find its place in the hearts of each generation." Fairy tales help us cross yet another boundary as they "carry away the young from the common sense of a protestant and capitalist reality into [Cinderella's] irresponsible romance" (HD 2.6.39–41). Driven to such "irresponsibility" by the demands of a culture whose value-system is increasingly defined by money, poets turn away with children and believers in other worlds to "some outcast area of the psyche itself, of a repressed content," a reality denied by those who will not accept it, "a 'they,' those who do not understand, who misjudge." Duncan reminds us that Hermes, god of poets, is "hermetic—hidden, sealed, occult, a messenger" (HD 2.2.16, 25, 34).

The fact that the stuff of such lore and of such poetry is a "repressed content" calls to mind Duncan's parallel interest, dating to his teen years, in psychology, especially the work of Sigmund Freud. In his belief that the poet does not initiate themes but recognizes them, that the poem compels the poet, Duncan found a kindred spirit in Freud. Like Duncan, Freud was fascinated by the artist's ability to work more than he knew. While Duncan quarrels with Freud's term "the unconscious," since any idea must be expressed in words, images, or dreams that are by definition part of our consciousness, they agree in principle and Freud remains a strong influence for Duncan: "I would still take Freud to be my master in his profound sense of the nature and operations of language. His chapter on 'The Dream Work' remains, for me, a primary insight disclosing the Poetic Mind" (FC 231). Attention to the "latent" content and to "mis-takes" characterizes both Freud's therapy and Duncan's poetry.

More "traditional" theories of mysticism enter into the weave of Duncan's work. Jewish mysticism, he said in an informative interview devoted to the subject, has been an "ongoing study" (Kamenetz 6), and was a major influence in the book *Letters.* Duncan has studied the lore, especially the *Zohar,* as well as the scholarship, most notably Gershom Scholem's *Major Trends in Jewish Mysticism.* Drawn to the Chassidic masters' belief in "the Hidden Zaddik, the divine wisdom that

the least of men may be illumined by" (FC 24), Duncan finds in their
work two powerful sources, in the Kabbalah's focus on language itself
as a source of creation, so that inspired meditation on the actual letters
of the Torah can release their creative powers, and in the doctrine of
correspondence—"As above, so below"—which Duncan had also en-
countered in his parents' Christian hermeticism. (See the Kamenetz
interview, passim.)

That hermeticism, of course, profoundly influenced the young poet
and opened his horizons to such an eclectic array of readings and faiths
in the first place. His accounts from memory of the young boy waiting
in the anteroom, listening to the adults reading behind the curtain,
testify to his lasting fascination with the occult. Just as he was awakening into language, glimpses from the adult world hinted at the hin-
terlands of the psyche. "The quest for meanings was a vital need in life
that one recognized in romance . . . By associations, by metaphor, by
likeness of the part, by fitting as part of a larger figure, by interlinking
of members, by share, by equation, by correspondence, by reason, by
contrast, by opposition, by pun or rime, by melodic coherence—what
might otherwise have seemed disparate things of the world as Chaos
were brought into a moving, changing, eternal, interweaving fabric of
the world as Creation. It was the multiplicity of meanings at play that
I loved" (HD 1.5.16).

The most sustained appearance of hermetic themes in Duncan's work
is *Adam's Way: A Play upon Theosophical Themes* (RB 127–63), virtually
a closet drama that specifically appeals to "only the man of childish
imagination" (128). In the course of the action, Dragons, Angels, and
"Tree-Shadows" contend in "an astral forest" and later in "the Garden
of Yahweh" as Adam and Erda-Eve come slowly into the questionable
gift of self-consciousness. Vague memories, still fading, of another
world "before Atlantis fell" evoke Duncan's early dream, and contrast
sharply with the heavy materialism of this world in which "Everything
they think / materializes. The Sun / they've thought a physical thing,
/ a burning mass. . . . / And Paradise, that was a bubble where images
whirld, / they burst in order to know it all" (131). The angel Samael
is a "demon" because he inflicts the curse of the self upon Adam,
whereas the angel Michael, "a daimon," presents the Sun's instruction,
"When from your self you are undone / What thou truly art will be
begun" (144). In this reenactment of "the grievous knowledge" of
Eden, his parents' religion's insistence on self-transcendence and on
obedience to mystery is almost too baldly stated.

Duncan is fully aware that such books as Madame Blavatsky's *Isis*

Unveiled or *The Secret Doctrine* are "beyond the dictates of reason," a "mess of astrology, alchemy, numerology, magic orders, neo-Platonic, kabbalistic and Vedic systems combined, confused, and explained," yet he insists that "her sense binds: that until man lives once more in these awes and consecrations, these obediences to what he does not know but feels, until he takes new thought in what he has discarded, he will not understand what he is" (HD 1.5.9–10). In an age that has declared the visionary trance as something out of bounds, irrational, Duncan insists on new ratios, relationships that answer felt needs. This heterodox worldview is, in his word, syncretic, accepting *Leaves of Grass* and the Bible on equal terms (Kamenetz 10), excluding nothing that could provide evidence of "the real" and enriching the poet's sense of poetry's possibilities.

Whitman

"It is significant that Shakespeare, Emerson, and Whitman are primaries for me," Duncan writes, "even as they were primaries in my parents' literature and also in their religion, for they took Shakespeare, Emerson, and Whitman to belong to their Hermetic and Rosicrucian tradition" (FC 224). He could easily have included Blake and Shelley,[2] also generative presences in his work, so that much of what is said here about Whitman and then Dante applies equally to these other authors of what Duncan terms "world poems, in which the passionate experience of the poet and the passionate experience of the world are identified" (FC 124). "Folks expect of the poet," Whitman wrote in his 1855 preface, "to indicate the path between reality and their souls." Citing this passage early in *The H. D. Book* (1.2.33), Duncan takes him at his word, taking him as well as Blake, or Dante, or Milton, "as gospels of Poetry . . . to testify to and in that to enter into the reality of a divine history within what men call history" (FC 44). In addition to "The Adventure of Whitman's Line," Duncan's resounding testimony to his own attraction to Whitman is the eloquent essay "Changing Perspectives in Reading Whitman": "Writing or reading, where words pass into this commanding music, I found a presence of person more commandingly real than what I thought to be my person before; Whitman or Shakespeare presenting more of what I was than I was" (FC 179). Like Whitman, Duncan is large and contains multitudes. He fulfills the serious office of the Romantic poet, searching out forms commensurate with the intrusion of disturbances that enter the poem.

One such disturbance strongly parallel in each man's work is his grappling with the meaning of America, not only as a political entity but as the generative source for poetic and personal endeavor. Undoubtedly the native American literary line seeks the basis of poetry in antipoetic or unpoetic material and in the creative potential of mundane subjects, and Duncan centers his affinity in Whitman's loving embrace of the particulars of American life: "In the very place where often contemporary individualism finds identity most lost, Whitman takes the ground of his identity and person: in the 'particulars and details magnificently moving in vast masses.' He saw Democracy not as an intellectual ideal but as an intuition of a grander and deeper reality potential in Man's evolution" (FC 191). Reading Whitman, Duncan enters this line of felt presences, though in Duncan's cosmology evil is more prevalent than Whitman's transcendentalism allowed. Whitman's projection in *Democratic Vistas* was toward a future, ideal America envisioned as a conjunction of a "new earth and a new man." Duncan, whose "Man's Fulfillment in Order and Strife" draws heavily upon *Democratic Vistas* (as well as upon Dante), takes up the order of the present.

Like Whitman, Duncan is preoccupied with the place of the creative individual in society, but with the nation's full entrance into Vietnam in the 1960s, the dualism inherent in the meaning of America asserts itself. "In our poetic tradition, our conscience as poets, we inherit a vision not only of the potentialities for good latent in the entity of these States, but also of the profound potentialities for evil. I drew not only upon the current of my own feeling as my vision sprang into life for me, sensing deeply the threat of a terror to come beyond the terrors we know in what the Vietnamese suffered—I mean the terror we must have in so far as we remain 'American' in America's crimes—but also upon my studies of how America had been seen by poets I recognized as inspired visionaries" (FC 131). In "The Fire: Passages 13," Duncan cites *The Eighteenth Presidency,* in which Whitman castigates the proslavery movement and the tumultuous political situation during the 1856 presidential campaign. The text and spirit of Whitman's essay enter Duncan's poem, establishing a synchronous field with twentieth century politics. Whitman's warning against Fillmore and Buchanan as "two dead corpses" parallels Duncan's censure of the demotic evil of Eisenhower, Nixon, and Goldwater.

The treatment becomes increasingly strident in the later *Passages,* most notably "Up Rising: Passages 25" and "The Soldiers: Passages 26," both unrelenting in their contempt for the Permanent War Economy. The latter evokes Whitman's words in bitter irony:

> *"The United States themselves are essentially the greatest poem".?*
> Then America, the secret union of all states of Man,
>   waits, hidden and challenging, in the hearts of the Viet Cong.
> *"The Americans of all nations at any time upon the earth,"*
>   Whitman says—the libertarians of the spirit, the
>   devotées of Man's commonality.
>
> (BB 113)

Duncan holds a far less sanguine view of America than Whitman, but his desire to call up its presence, despite inherent contradictions, is equally imperative. At the political level Duncan can work less on faith than Whitman, and he is too honest to fool himself that Whitman's egalitarian optimism remains viable for *all* men in the twentieth century: "Totalism—*ensemblism*—is haunted when we return to it today in the dark monstrosities of socialistic and democratic totalitarianism" (FC 168). Yet man's potential for world order sustains Duncan as it sustained Whitman, because "underlying these United States and this America, comes a mystery of 'America' that belongs to dream and desire and the reawakening of earliest oneness with all peoples—at last, the nation of Mankind at large" (FC 171).

The difficulty for the contemporary poet is generated by the creative contradiction between Whitman's sense of political and personal fulfillment, and Duncan's realization that he comes too late in history merely to recapitulate the older poet's stance. "How far from Whitman's sense of what it means, of filling and fullness, my own poetic apocalyptic sense of signs and meanings fulfilled is" (FC 181). That tension informs his "Poem Beginning with a Line by Pindar," which contrasts Whitman's feeling for Lincoln in the great elegy "When Lilacs Last in the Dooryard Bloom'd" with the line of Presidents since, "idiots fumbling at the bride's door." Struggling to maintain some sense of continuity, he turns "toward the old poets / . . . to their faltering, / their unaltering wrongness that has style" (OF 63). "Glorious mistake!" he terms two of Whitman's statements in the 1855 preface: "The theme is creative and has vista," and "He is the president of regulation." He was mistaken in the specific light of historical realities, but the mistake is glorious in Duncan's sense that the spirit of the proposition creates a compelling moment that can inspire later poets. Whitman had argued that poetry is generated in the painful throes of "doubts, suspense . . . surrounding war and revolution."[3] Duncan accedes in this, finding that poetry issues from and entertains repeated patterns of "order and disorder" (FC 140). Composing a "true epithalamium," in which discordant elements enter, redefine the boundaries of the poem, and "dance together" (FC 27), remains for Duncan the high task of Romantic poets, a company he willingly enters with Whitman.

Composing such poetry demanded a poetic revolution, as Whitman discovered an expansive form to express his unconventional subjects, themes, and ideas. *Leaves of Grass* is the archetypal organic poem, its open and processual method as much a part of the subject matter as its content. The immediate presence of Whitman's poet-protagonist informs *Leaves of Grass,* and its continual evolution justifies the growth of his book, not by additions but by organic evolution, each edition one possible statement of the ever-evolving whole, the ensemble. In Duncan's apt description, *Leaves* was "not a blueprint but an evolution of spirit in terms of variety and a thicket of potentialities" (FC 166). *The Opening of the Field* announced Duncan's allegiance to open form, and it should come as no surprise that in the course of its writing, "*Leaves of Grass* was kept as a bedside book" (FC 190). Significantly, Duncan's sense of the poem as a field of composition in which the poet becomes a unifying register of perception parallels Whitman's fictive strategy.

The large form each poet works toward is the result of a mutual, organic coinherence of all the parts of the poem.[4] Where Whitman turned to the "ensemble" as the only structure large enough to suggest the comprehensiveness of his vision, Duncan has spoken of his poetry as a collage in which a number of new elements enter the poem to create new complexes of meaning. *Passages* and *The Structure of Rime,* in particular, are so expansive and receptive that they welcome the varied intrusions of the poet's consciousness, laying out before him a polysemous correspondence of elements (BB x) both known and hinted, which force the reader to reassess what unity means. The premise of incompleteness, the weight of the "never achiev'd poem,"[5] is a heavy burden indeed, but one which Robert Duncan, of all our contemporary poets, is best able to carry to fruition.

Dante

Where Whitman serves as "the grand proposer of questions not to be settled, the poet of unsettling propositions," Duncan notes that "Whitman nowhere presents the architectural ordering of universe and spirit that Dante presents" (FC 164). Duncan's poetics of encyclopedic inclusiveness draws as much from Dante's hierarchic system and religious faith as from Whitman's open road and his barbaric yawp. Indeed, given Duncan's emphasis on strife and disorder as necessary parts of the process of a larger, evolutionary (but not necessarily ameliorative) order, his attraction to Dante and Milton can be seen as an inevitable balance to his attraction to Whitman. As with Whitman, Duncan testifies to his allegiance to Dante with eloquent prose—*The Sweetness and Greatness of Dante's Divine Comedy* as well as references in *The H. D. Book* and "Man's Fulfillment in Order and Strife"—and with frequent allusions in the poetry. Further, he has two sequences of Dante poems: a series of five sonnets, three in *Roots and Branches* (122–24) and two more in *Bending the Bow* (3, 5); and the much more extended *Dante Études* in *Ground Work* (discussed in chapter 8, below).

Duncan's preface to the *Dante Études* declares the immediate importance of Dante, not only to his own work but to the twentieth century. "His is not a mind researcht in the lore of another time, for me, but immediate, everlastingly immediate, to the presence of the idea of Poetry. . . . I draw my 'own' thought in reading Dante as from a wellspring" (GW 94). Once again, the synchronous field of poetry provides an enabling presence, memorably phrased here as "translated powers."

Duncan reads Dante at several levels, citing a telling excerpt from a Dante letter to his patron, Can Grande: "The sense of this work is not simple, but on the contrary, it may be called *polysemous,* that is to say, 'of more senses than one'" (FC 143). In his introduction to *Bending the Bow,* Duncan reminds us of Dante's word here and its importance to his own poetry, taking "each thing of the composition as generative of meaning, a response to and a contribution to the building form" (BB ix). As he talks about the four levels of Dante's work—literal, allegorical, moral, and anagogical—Duncan stresses their cooperation rather than their separateness.

Dante's themes hold a lasting appeal as well. In the first place, they are strongly grounded in his own life experience: "Dante, I think, incorporates the actualities of history, of his own life and of the history of man, as essential to his poem, because it is essential in his religion that God was actually and historically incarnate" (FC 144). In Dante as well as in Whitman, Duncan finds a predecessor who confronts his own time and place in his work, and such inspirations loom large in his own poetry, especially in *Passages.* Noting that Dante's *De Vulgari Eloquentia* names three themes for poetry, "prowess of arms, the fire of

love, and the direction of the will," Duncan characteristically refigures
the orders in an active engagement with his master. For prowess of
arms he reads safety, and asserts, "Our safety lay in our imagination of
what man was, not in the defense but in the opening of our minds.
Our prowess must lie now not in defeating the enemy but in the more
problematic, the longer effort to understand our common humanity
with him" (HD Day Book 9, 11). Taking his orders as they arise in a
time as tumultuous as Dante's thirteenth century, Duncan posits a rev-
olutionary role for the poet. Just as Dante "betrayed" Florence, Duncan
opposes his own government, "those who govern the United States in
the name of private enterprise and properties against communal goods
and who are engaged in a disastrous struggle for domination of other
nations against their counterparts in Russia and in China. We live
today, as Dante lived in the thirteenth century and in Florence, in a
crisis of just these three worthiest subjects [safety, love, and virtue]
that must have their definitions not in our personal interests, or we
find ourselves at war against the very safety we would fight for, but in
our common humanity (HD 2.5, part 2.50–51). Those who would
disallow politics in poetry are as bad as those who would demand it.
Poetry must follow its own orders and so cannot serve as propaganda,
but at the same time it must be rooted in "the living body and passion
of Man in the actual universe" (FC 144).

The richness of Dante's language, finally, inspires Duncan's admi-
ration. "The beauty of sound is, for Dante, first and last, the essence
of his art" (FC 152). Duncan's poetry, we shall see, is also highly musical, attentive to vowels and pitch and painstakingly presented on the
page to alert the reader to it *as music,* and such poetry derives from
Dante's mellifluous terza rima as well as from Pound and Stravinsky.
Dante's great poem provides a warning, however, of "the great temp-
tation of all true poets," that is, "to be so enraptured by the beauty of
the language" that they "lose the intent of the whole, the working of
the power towards the fullness in meaning of its form" (FC 151). Thus,
Virgil must repeatedly awaken Dante to his task, calling him away
from the temptations of story, of image, and language that arrest his
progress in his journey, just as "in the midst of our all too human delite
in whatever partakes of heavenly beauty there is danger if we take no
thought of God and our eternal life" (FC 156).

Such language, characteristic of Duncan's writing about Dante, emphasizes the importance of poetry and his high seriousness toward his

art. Both poets, of course, are multifaceted and have rich veins of humor. But where Dante dedicates his art to his God, Duncan dedicates his art to the service of his Master of Rime. Duncan's poetry, too, enters into the strife of our times, charged with a necessary task. "If we are so upon the brink of the destruction not only of political orders and of civilizations but of the potentiality of world order itself—for that is the nightmare content of our times— . . . then we are in such a perversion of government that no man who means good can be a good citizen." Further, that nightmare has infected our language itself, the poet's very medium: "If our manner of speech has come, as it has, to be so much a cover that for the sake of freedom men are drafted against their will; for the sake of peace, armed men and tanks fight in our streets; and for the sake of the good life, the resources of our land are ruthlessly wasted, and waterways and air polluted, then we need a new manner of speaking" (FC 119). These are hard words for hard times, spat into the face of an age that actually believes that "poetry makes nothing happen." Something is happening in Duncan's work, and a major source of its inspiration is Dante, one of the suns of Duncan's poetic cosmology.

Linguists, Psychologists, Philosophers, Scientists

The neatly dovetailing quality of this chapter's sections breaks down here in the face of Duncan's encyclopedic eclecticism. He reads widely and incorporates, directly or indirectly, a great deal of what he reads into his writing, as even a glance at the "Notes" to *Bending the Bow* reveals, ranging as it does from the *Oxford English Dictionary* to Truman Michelson's *The Owl Sacred Pack of Fox Indians,* published by the Bureau of American Ethnology, to D. P. Walker's *Spiritual and Demonic Magic from Ficino to Campanella,* to an article in *Scientific American.*

Duncan has long been interested in science, which he calls our "contemporary mythmaking": "Our theogony now is our science. I'm reading that all the time. It must be a myth. I mean, it again is a proposition that goes towards reality" (Mesch 87, 86). His reading ranges from the art historian Siegfried Giedion's discussion of technology and organicism, *Mechanization Takes Command* (1948); to Wolfgang Kohler's analysis of fields, vectors, and forces in art, *The Place of Value in a World of Facts* (1938); to Richard Grossinger's uncategorizable *Solar Journal: Oecological Sections,* for which Duncan wrote an introductory note; to Murray Gell-Mann's theories of subatomic particles, Duncan's use of which is discussed in chapter 7; to many, many more, including the cultural anthropology and linguistic theories of Edward Sapir and Benjamin Lee Whorf.

In the work of Sapir and Whorf, he found the hypothesis that a person's native language defines the way he or she perceives and interprets the world. As Whorf puts it in "Science and Linguistics" (1940), "We dissect nature along lines laid down by our native languages."[6] But Duncan pushed farther than this, into their investigations into the nature of language and its effect on culture. Both men were eclectic and brilliant, working from hunches and intuitive insights toward large patterns and implications that both startled and often frightened their professional colleagues. Whorf, in fact, never earned an advanced degree and worked as a fire safety engineer for an insurance company his entire adult life. A self-described visionary whose interest in linguistics had religious roots, he began his career inspired by the hypothesis that letters have inherent meaning in themselves, and late in his career, as he reports in "Language, Mind, and Reality" (1941), was still investigating "the psychic ring" of vowels in laboratory tests.[7] Duncan's continuing interest in the tone leading of vowels could only have been stimulated by such work, and his early interest in the mystical nature of letters parallels Whorf's. Sapir was himself a poet and studied music as well, and his late published papers have been called unrhymed poetry. His concerns with a language's phonetic groundwork and morphological peculiarities likewise provided Duncan with theoretical bases for his own work. Sapir's *Language* (1921) traced poetry's origin in all cultures to "the singing voice and the measure of the dance," and argued that "style is not an absolute, a something that is to be imposed on the language from Greek or Latin models, but merely the language itself, running in its natural grooves."[8] Speaking of his interest in both men in an interview, Duncan discusses "the submeaning level" of the syllable, "the intoxicating spell that comes out of that thing that happened to that syllable" (Bowering and Hogg, n.p.), an aspect of poetry and linguistics still in need of much analysis.

Sapir and Whorf linked cultural anthropology and linguistics with psychology and philosophy, and Duncan's interests here are again wide-ranging and overlapping. They include not only Plato and the pre-Socratics, especially Heraclitus and Empedocles, but extend all the way to contemporary writers. Sigmund Freud's theories on "the dream work," we have already seen, reinforced Duncan's ideas about the creative process and the limits of common sense. Freud's insistence on paying attention to one's "mistakes" similarly enters Duncan's creative method in his attentiveness to the significance of the immediate present. "As in the Freudian reading of the dream, all the parts belong, no member is to be dismissed as trivial or mistaken. Mistakes themselves mark the insistence of meanings in other meanings; more is present than we would rightly want to take it was present. For Freud, not only dream but waking reality is not meaningless or formless but to be read in signs. The numen commands or beckons from every stone" (FC 47; see also 33–34). Duncan's willingness to follow the lure of the poem into any area is grounded in his reading of Freud. A very different theory is Jean Piaget's psychology of process, yet Duncan draws on its congenial aspects as well. Noting in an interview that Freud is "eighteenth century minded" in having preconceived configurations such as the Oedipus complex that he applied to specific cases, Duncan calls attention to Piaget's emphasis on process: "The fundamental fact is the unrolling of the construct itself, this derollment itself, what's before you as you're writing. You don't think it out, it unfolds & develops before you. . . . The structures are not given in advance nor is the human mind or the exterior world as such. Nor do we perceive them or organize them. They construct themselves" (Abbott and Shurin, *Soup* 43). Duncan's conviction that reality is constantly in process, changing and evolving, insists upon an openness to experience and a poetry that is likewise open and inclusive.

An even greater influence on Duncan's work in this regard is William James's *Principles of Psychology* (1890), with its theme of the fluidity of consciousness. For James with his great interest in the "penumbra" of experience, "life is at the transitions." As he says in "A World of Pure Experience," "Our fields of experience have no more definite boundaries than have our fields of view. Both are fringed forever by a *more* that continuously develops and that continuously supersedes them as life proceeds."[9] For Duncan as for James, life is at the edge, at the point of relationship, surprise, novelty—at the transgression of boundaries. Conceiving the universe as a constant rhythm between order and disorder, both (with Alfred North Whitehead and John Dewey) maintain that order develops. Rejecting the extreme poles of a world of mere flux without any stability and a static world without crisis, such a worldview embraces the moment of pas-

sage as that of most intense life. Appropriately, Duncan's major ongoing poem is entitled "The Passages Poems." James's insistence on
inclusiveness, on an acceptance of "the total reality," is also important
to Duncan: "It is 'the total world which *is*' that concerns James; and
in his sense that What Is is multifarious, in his insistence upon the
many strands we must come to see before consciousness have something
like the fullness demanded by What Is, James is kin to Emerson before
him and to Dewey and Whitehead after" (HD 2.5, part 1.337–38).
Of this constellation of influences, Whitehead's theories are the single
most important for Duncan's poetics and consequently are discussed at
some length in chapter 3, below.

Emerson could have been discussed in tandem with Whitman, but
Emerson's ideas are far more important than his poetry, both for Duncan and for American culture at large. As important as Whitman is to
him, Duncan announced at a 1979 gathering of scholars, "I am an
Emersonian poet." The embarrassed titters emanating from a few of
these students of modern poetry provided yet another indication that
the poet is better educated than some of his critics. Emerson's ground
work feeds the roots of Whitman, Dewey, James, and Whitehead
alike, and for them he is not the clubby Victorian sage but a profoundly
anguished thinker. Duncan read Emerson in 1946 or 1947, and three
essays—"Experience," "Dreams," and "Self-Reliance"—were especially
important to him. Now as then, Duncan remains an aggressive reader.

"Trust thyself;" Emerson writes there: "every heart vibrates to that iron
string." . . . "Trust no conviction," I would write back: "least of all thy 'self';
mistrust thy self; every heart vibrates from that iron string. Yet upon this
string alone you must make the sound come true." Today, in 1979, reading
that essay, I find again how Emersonian my spirit is. All of experience seems
my trust fund to me; I must cultivate the mistrust that alone can give contrast
and the needed inner tension for vital interest. In this, I stand almost heret-
ically disposed to Olson's insistence on Melville's sense of inner catastrophe
against the Emersonian bliss. But, if there is bliss acknowledged in Emerson,
I read my Emerson dark.

(FC 226)

Duncan's Contemporaries

Finally, Duncan's work must be read in terms of the poetry of his
time, a dynamic and exciting era with multiple derivations of its own.

As I noted in my preface, Duncan will seem incomplete to readers unaware of his contemporaries. He addresses the importance of context in talking to Ekbert Faas: "It had been awfully important to me to feel that Denise Levertov and Robert Creeley and Charles Olson and myself were a kind of movement and that they took care of a lot of areas that I even by temperament wouldn't be likely to cover. . . . And in a group, of course, you can assume that your reader is also going to read Olson. So you can save a lot of time, because all you have to do is take a potshot that hits off against a facet of Charles Olson and he covers miles of territory of what you are. . . . But you only have to make the slightest distinctions and your reader will realize how a lot of things are disposed. And then in the composition of a poem you don't have to do lots of explication" (60–61). The reader who regards such demands as a compliment rather than a burden is Duncan's ideal reader. To what other should a poet be expected to address himself?

The twentieth century has seen two generations of poets come to maturity, and our inadequate critical vocabulary has labeled them chronologically as Moderns and Contemporaries (or worse, Postmoderns). This is hardly the place to establish better terms, but when the critics catch up to the poets Hugh Kenner's term, "the Pound Era," will do as well as most. Pound, for better or worse, was at the center of everything vital. In 1937, eighteen-year old Robert Duncan was encountering Stravinsky, Picasso, Pound, Stein, Cummings, Williams, Joyce and the other "modernists," who "opened up a world of what writing could mean and, indeed, of a life way, outside the bounds of my college courses and the discussion groups of my fellow students, where only *Ulysses* and *The Waste Land* gave any hint of what the 'modern' might be, of the shift from the idea of writing, and especially poetry, as an expression or cultivation of sensibility as such, to that of writing as meaning realized as it was 'made' or 'discovered' in the process of invention and experiment" ("Reading Zukofsky" 422).[10]

Such a charged excitement drives Duncan's voracious appetite for art, music, and literature. The *H. D. Book* is a long testimony to his active engagement with H. D.'s work but also to that of her contemporaries and her predecessors. For her, as for Duncan, earlier writers are "previous incarnations of the spirit at work": "These poems where many persons from many times and many places begin to appear—as in *The Cantos, The Waste Land, Finnegans Wake,* the War Trilogy, and *Paterson*—are poems of a world-mind in process" (HD 1.6.66). More than a mere antiquarian trip, he continues, the poet's search for such "enduring terms for the renewal of poetry in his own time" is an imperative in the face of "the seemingly triumphant reality of the War and State." Poets such as Pound, H. D., Williams, and Lawrence are quite literally heroes in seeing "literature as a text of the soul in its search for fulfillment in life" and in taking "the imagination as a primary instinctual authority. The generative imagination Pound called it" (HD 2.1.113). Nonetheless, Duncan insists he is not a modernist, reading modernism ultimately as an extension of an unbroken continuity from the Romantic period of the nineteenth century (Faas 82).

Duncan brings a similar orneriness to his reading of his contemporaries, and he alludes as easily to Jackson Pollock and John Cage as to Picasso and Stravinsky. Most instructive, though, is his relationship to Charles Olson and Louis Zukofsky. As Duncan told Linda Hamalian, "Olson found Zukofsky intolerable and couldn't read a line of him if he tried. And of course, it also went the other way around" (91–92). Duncan's ability to draw fruitfully from both poets testifies to his openness and eclecticism as well as anything. (A counterargument would be that this is a sign of an inability to discriminate, but no one familiar with Duncan's pithy opinions would ever accuse him of *that*. Our concern here is what does interest him, not what does not.) He sees the two as "antibodies" of each other, contrasting Zukofsky's fineness of distinction with Olson's sweeping inspirations (Bowering and Hogg, n.p.). His argument that his own work must be read in the context of others' work arises most clearly and cogently in this relationship. "In relation to each I was to be heretical—for in the face of Zukofsky's process of stripping to essentials, I was working toward a proliferation of meanings; and in the face of Olson's drive toward the primordial roots, I was working from interpretations of the text. The two could not read each other; but it was my sense early in the 1950s that the test of our sources in Poetry must be in the reading of them both as primaries" ("Reading Zukofsky" 421–22).

Duncan draws as easily upon Olson's 1950 proposition of projective verse as upon Pound's 1910 proposition of the ideogram. This entire discussion of his sources only begins to encompass his eclectic derivations, and hardly hints at his ability to reject baleful aspects while incorporating what he wants. Duncan was certainly no slavish follower of anyone, as can be seen in his discerning use of both Zukofsky and Pound. His essay on reading Zukofsky notes that "A–8" praises Stalin and Pound's *Cantos* celebrate Mussolini, and concludes, "Whatever a poem meant in its truth of particulars it was not a political directive.

The truth of a poem was the truth of what was felt in the course of the poem, not the truth of a proposition in whatever political or religious persuasion outside the poem" (426–27). Duncan's embrace of the occult from the Zohar to Madame Blavatsky, of Whitman and Dante, Milton and Blake, Olson and Zukofsky, serves to bring them all into the present moment. While he calls himself a derivative poet, his penetrating readings of his predecessors generate contemporary visions, Emersonian prospects of discovery and renewal. "Turn back the pages as they will," he tells us, "every part of man's story has been re-informed by the creative genius of his own present moment" (FC 36). In his combination of tradition with presence, Duncan attends to the multiple processes of poetic apprehension, "not to praise or to appraise, but to bear testimony to the enduring resource" ("Reading Zukofsky" 427).

Chapter Three
Poetics

Just as the divorce rate indicates that many people are more interested in the idea of marriage than in an actual marriage, many literary critics today are more interested in the idea of literature than in actual stories and poems, which, like actual marriages, tend to have their own unique problems and pleasures. While this preference is generally lamentable and, one dearly hopes, passing, nonetheless the study of poetics—the theory of poetry, how poems work—can be very helpful, especially with a poet like Duncan, who is very articulate when discussing his own poetics.

"Poetry is language that becomes so excited that it is endlessly creative of message," he tells Bowering and Hogg, so that "you never, in one sense, get it, and you always get sent by it" (n.p.). Such a promise of incompleteness, of poetry as "the intellectual adventure of not knowing" (FC 46), informs Duncan's ideal of poetry. Without an understanding of that basic proposition readers of his work will be continually confused and frustrated.

A full apprehension of Duncan's poetry demands attention to two warring elements, an impassioned content and a delight in the pleasures of language—sound, rhythm, rhyme—for their own sake. While Duncan has rightly criticized modern scholars for not attending to the crisis of the content, at the same time a failure to attend to the music of the poem will similarly destroy the poetic experience. Duncan has repeatedly emphasized the importance of the physical body in his poetry's generation and in its reading, and his 1955 essay "Poetry before Language" clearly celebrates "the happy concourse and democracy of what we do not mind," the wordless life of "hand, arm, leg, foot, finger, stomach, bowels, liver, heart, lungs, brain, skin and bone" before brain took over (FC 60–61). As when a small child approaches from behind pushing a grocery cart, anyone whose tingling Achilles tendons have alerted adrenal glands and leg muscles knows that the body has ways of knowing that do not involve brain. Poetry before

words, then, "would not allow the brain to falsify what it was in giving
it a word or a 'meaning.' . . . In one kind of dancing the hand and the
eye danced together. Thus the hand 'saw' the stones and sticks, and
the eye 'felt' them. The foot danced with the sight and the feel which
measured the ground and made space, and the eye heard accurately the
measures on the ground as the accents of the tread and the numbers of
the steps or stops and the stretches or durations or silences between
steps and stops" (61–62). Many readers find such an irrationalist statement unacceptable, but Duncan is absolutely serious in insisting on an
attention to all the processes of the poem, by both poet and reader, and
an understanding of his idea of a poem is essential to an apprehension
of his work.

In effect, poetry is an activity, a process in which the poet is permitted to participate. "Love, desire, and beauty, in the poet's Theogony, precede mankind. They were once forces that came to be
forms. . . . It is the virtue of words that what were forces become
meanings and seek form. Cosmic powers appear as presences and even
as persons of inner being to the imagination" (HD 1.3.70). *Virtue,*
here, means "power" rather than, as more commonly, "goodness."
Words embody these cosmic powers in a poetry whose apprehension
involves both senses of the word: grasping its meaning, and also awe,
fear in the presence of such cosmic powers.

Duncan makes unabashedly large claims for poetry as a metaphysical
experience, while at the same time he downplays his personal role as a
poet: "Poems are for me only occasions of Poetry, of coming into this
consciousness of things as potentials for making a universe real—celebrating, is it? or evoking? Of singing and dancing What Is" (HD Day
Book 10). Vision is neither earned nor deserved, but rather is "a grace
recognized by the writer in the reality of things" (FC 25). The poet's
own life and achievement are insignificant in this larger, nonhumanist
universe, except insofar as they become common, communal. Duncan
explicitly rejects an art of values ("the painting as culture-commodity
or the poem as an item of education") and of aesthetic qualities ("the
painting or poem as a paradigm of the Beautiful"), instead taking his
stand for art as "primarily the means of human experience . . . to become communal and actual. Our own lives, like our dreams, are fleet-
ing and insubstantial, unless they cease to be our own and are shared,
created in the medium of images or words, delivered over into the
commons of man's life and dreams" (HD Day Book 5).

In spite of its insistent high seriousness, Duncan's poetry remains
playful and spirited, as in the teasing whimsy of the opening of "Where
It Appears: Passages 4" (BB 15):

> I'd cut the warp
> to weave that web
>
> in the air
>
> and here
>
> let image perish in image,
>
> leave writer and reader
>
> up in the air
>
> to draw
>
> momentous
>
> inconclusions,
>
> ropes of the first water
> returnd by a rhetoric
>
> the rain swells.

Although Duncan's lines tease us with our "momentous inconclusions," his difficult, expansive, receptive poetry is at the same time
highly serious. For Duncan, "The poetic imagination faces the challenge of finding a structure that will be the complex story of all the
stories felt to be true, a myth in which something like the variety of
man's experience of what is real may be contained" (FC 6). In fulfilling
the mission to tell us the truth as a new truth, Duncan demands of us
a new understanding of poetry, insisting that we rely less upon intel-
lection and drawing heavily upon Alfred North Whitehead's cosmology. At the beginning of *Maximus Poems V,* after noting "Whitehead's
important corollary: that no event / is not penetrated, in intersection
or collision with, an eternal / event," Charles Olson observes, "The
poetics of such a situation / are yet to be found out."[1]

Toward the end of finding out such a poetics, the rest of this chapter examines two of the most challenging formal aspects of Duncan's poetry, which can be linked under the descriptive term "unfinished": first, in that it is unpolished, largely unrevised, since his poetics insist that poetry as a matter of inspiration calls for vision, not revision; second, in that it is never completed or perfected. Both notions violate traditional views of poetry, and both are generated by the same concept of poetry, one with roots in ancient poetries and more recent branches in modern romanticism. Duncan's eclectic and intellectual poetry is informed by a profound and ultimately teleological worldview.

Barbara Herrnstein Smith defines *closure* as a "sense of stable conclusiveness, finality, or 'clinch,'" as "a modification of structure that makes *stasis,* or the absence of further continuation, the most probable succeeding event." Stasis is the very quality Duncan insists he must avoid. Closure quickly boils down to a matter of teleology, as Smith observes: "A poem is, in a sense, caused by its own effects. That is, the poet is constantly making choices that are determined by his sense of their ultimate effectiveness. . . . It must often happen, in fact, that the *donnée* of poem is its conclusion, that the poet began with the end, and that what the reader perceives as an ending determined by the poem's thematic structure may, from the poet's point of view, have been what determined that structure in the first place."[2] While this sounds like the Poe of "The Philosophy of Composition," it is not a description of what Duncan is doing. He has repeatedly said his "Passages" will never end and that all his poems are part of one field of poetry. Far from beginning with his conclusion, Duncan insists upon "momentous inconclusions." The inconclusiveness *is* momentous. This new poetry is expansive in form and receptive to experience, recognizing that only such qualities will accommodate the process of things as they are. Only such a poetry, paradoxically, will give us an effectively teleological poem.

Duncan's poetry is antiteleological only in a limited sense, that of its being "unfinished" as I have described it. However, Duncan's poetry and his statements about poetry manifest a firm belief in a design; the poetry is, then, teleological. It is perfecting rather than perfected, and calls for a reexamination of our ideas of art and order. The sense of order we find in Duncan resembles that of Whitehead, who maintains in *Process and Reality* that "Nature is never complete."[3] Duncan consequently has developed an evolutionary theory of art: "In writing I came to be concerned not with poems in themselves but with the life of poems as part of the evolving and continuing work of a poetry I could never complete—a poetry that had begun long before I was born and that extended beyond my own work in it. . . . My search for a poetry that was not to come to a conclusion, a mankind that was in process not in progress . . . leads me on to a view of language, world and order, as being in process, as immediate happening, evolving and perishing, without any final goal—the goal being in the present moment alone" (FC 113–14). Process, the opposite of stasis, is reality.

While common sense maintains a distinction between reality as that which is and that which becomes, Whitehead dissolves the distinction in his Ninth Category of Explanation: "That *how* an actual entity *becomes* constitutes *what* that actual entity *is;* so that the two descriptions of an actual entity are not independent. Its 'being' is constituted by its 'becoming.' This is the 'principle of process'" (PR 28). Consequently, the popular belief in a final order must be abandoned in favor of the possibility of different types of order. "This belief in a final order, popular in religious and philosophic thought, seems to be due to the prevalent fallacy that all types of seriality necessarily involve terminal instances" (PR 131). According to Whitehead, instead of rejecting what does not fit one's preconceptions, one should harmonize discordant elements. A literature that will not admit chaos cannot achieve such a harmony: "The right chaos, and the right vagueness, are jointly required for any effective harmony" (PR 132). Duncan accepts chance as opposed to reason's logic in "Passages: JAMAIS":

> "Reason being such always
>   men fail to understand"
> All ways   men fail to understand.
>
> Lovely, the Dreams and Chance encounters
> but Now   is wedded thruout to   the Intention of a Universe.
>   Verse,   linkt to the Idea of that Governance,
> moves "beyond"
>
> (GW 147)

Further, Heraclitus' word *logos* takes on a far larger meaning for which no single English word exists. G. S. Kirk suggests "measure," "the organized way in which all things work," "plan (in a non-teleological sense)," "rule," "law," or "formula of things."[4] In short, man must submit his will to order to a larger measure or order of nature. As a consequence, for Duncan, "Order can't possibly be threatened. Disorder is one of its terms. . . . The themes of possible disorder are interior and orderly to the poem."[5]

Language by itself is inadequate to express such reality, and requires imaginative participation of both writer and reader (both of whom are left up in the air in "Where It Appears," cited above). For Whitehead, a verbal statement is never the full expression of a proposition: "Meanings are incapable of accurate apprehension apart from a correspondingly accurate apprehension of the metaphysical background which the universe provides for them. But no language can be anything but elliptical, requiring a leap of the imagination to understand its meaning in its relevance to immediate experience" (PR 16). Modern criticism has widely recognized the problems of presenting meaning in language. "The language of literature," Whitehead observes, "breaks down precisely at the task of expressing in explicit form the larger generalities." The resolution of this problem, however, lies not in subjectivism or solipsism, but in a recognition that "every proposition proposing a fact must, in its complete analysis, propose the general character of the universe required for that fact" (PR 14). Nothing exists in static isolation. The universe is a field of relationships. Consequently, Duncan demands a new sense of meaning to correspond to his sense of the universe's orders: "There is not a phase of our experience that is meaningless, not a phrase of our communication that is meaningless. We do not make things meaningful, but in our making we work towards an awareness of meaning; poetry reveals itself to us as we obey the orders that appear in our work" (FC 82).

Whitehead uses the term *passage* to describe the operations of the process: "Objective identity requires integration of the many feelings of one object into the one feeling of that object. . . . Each actual entity is a cell with atomic unity. But in analysis it can only be understood as a process; it can only be felt as a process, that is to say, as in passage" (PR 265). While individual poems in Duncan's "Passages" may have "atomic unity,"[6] they are quite clearly meant to be experienced as parts of a process, one that is larger than the set of poems and larger, as Duncan says, "than my work in them." We cannot expect language to explain that which is beyond experience, but the process or passage of a particular experience can yield insights into an ultimate design. Because it "enacts in its order the order of first things," such a poetry "desires to penetrate the seeming of style and subject matter to that most real where there is no form that is not content, no content that is not form" (FC 81). Whitehead and Duncan do not doubt that design, and the implications of such a poetics are large.

Before turning to those implications, one must clarify the relation of Duncan's poetics and Whitehead's cosmology, using a brief but crucial description of *experience* that Whitehead accurately calls a simplification:

Any actual entity, which we will name A, feels other actual entities which we will name B, C, and D. Thus B, C, and D all lie in the actual world of A. But C and D may lie in the actual world of B, and are then felt by it; also D may lie in the actual world of C and be felt by it. This example might be simplified, or might be changed to one of any degree of complication. Now B, as an initial datum for A's feeling, also presents C and D for A to feel through its mediation. Also C, as an initial datum for A's feeling, also presents D for A to feel through its mediation. Thus, in this artificially simplified example, A has D presented for feeling through three distinct sources: (i) directly as a crude datum, (ii) by the mediation of B, and (iii) by the mediation of C. This three-fold presentation is D, in its function as an initial datum for A's feeling of it, so far as concerns the mediations of B *and* C. But of course, the artificial simplification of the medium to two intermediaries is very far from any real case. The medium between D and A consists of all those actual entities which lie in the actual world of A and not in the actual world of D. (PR 264)

Out of context this passage may seem cryptic, but it is at the heart of Duncan's poetic theory and practice, for it is the notion of the complicated interrelatedness of all experience that generates the concept of the poem as a field of activity which is entered by the poet. This entrance is momentary, a matter of "permission." It is quite literally a passage through experience, a paradoxical attempt to fix briefly ceaseless change, but with a new twist: Duncan admits the transitory, imperfect nature of the passage and records it as accurately as he can. Thus the poem appears unfinished in its lack of polish or conclusions, in order to reflect the nature of experience.

The overriding sense of an ultimate design or interrelated field is not vitiated simply because language cannot contain it. "Central to and defining the poetics I am trying to suggest here," Duncan writes, "is the conviction that the order man may contrive or impose upon the things about him or upon his own language is trivial beside the divine order or natural order he may discover in them" (FC 81–82). This new idea of order, of a Universal Law distinct from man's law, could not possibly be encapsulated in any one poem or series of poems, since "the truth we know is not of What Is, but of What Is Happening" (FC 46). It is a changing order growing out of process and thus experienced in parts of a poem or in sets of poems.

Unlike the modernist writer who sees a poem as a finished, intricately contrived creation, Duncan must accept the discord necessary for true harmony: "the work of art is itself the field we would render the truth of. Focusing in on the process itself as the field of the poem, the jarring discord must enter the composition" (FC 48–49). The mistakes and inattentions that Freud taught us to attend to are part of the experience of the poem and must not be excluded. The process is not a matter of mere chance, however, but of the "Creative Will that realizes Itself in Form evolving in the play of primordial patterns" (FC 34). Surrendering his personal will to that Creative Will in the appropriately named "Orders: Passages 24," Duncan puts aside "whatever I once served of the poet, master / of enchanting words and magics," instead looking "this time as you bid me to see" (BB 77). Belief in this kind of order recognizes that submission to order is the only real freedom, and that accurate attention to experience will lead to a passage to reality, as in "In the Place of a Passage 22":

> That Freedom and the Law are identical
> and are the nature of Man—Paradise

The seed I am knows only the green law of the tree into which
it sends out its roots, life and branches,

> unhinderd,   the vast universe
>   showing only its vast boundaries we imagine.

Grant me passages . . .

                                        (BB 74)

The allusion to Duncan's *Roots and Branches* serves to emphasize that all his poems derive from the same poetics, that they are interrelated and active in the one field of the poem. Shelley's great essay on the social and moral function of poetry speaks of "that great poem, which all poets, like the co-operating thoughts of one great mind, have built up since the beginning of the world,"[7] and to understand Duncan's sense of this poem we need to recognize the tradition in which he works. Duncan thinks of poetry as "a wrestling with Form to liberate Form" (FC 8). Even to speak of particular "Passages" as fragments of a larger whole would imply that the fragments could be pieced together to form a coherent object, rather than a coinherent experience without a distinction between subject and object, a "creation, creature, and creator coinherent in the one event" (FC 81).

Those who willfully read the fragmentation and discontinuity of much twentieth century literature as signs of the collapse of artistic imagination or of civilization itself are simply not attending to the literature and its processes. As Gabriel Josipovici argues in *The Lessons of Modernism*:

The principles of fragmentation and discontinuity, of repetition and spiral-ling, . . . do not reveal anything so banal as the final disintegration of the Western Imagination. What they perhaps reveal is the disintegration of a notion of Truth, and of the power of the intellect alone to discover that truth and embody it in works of art, which men had come to take for granted in the centuries following the Renaissance. The fragmented or spiralling work denies us the comfort of finding a centre, a single meaning, a speakable truth, either in works of art or in the world. In its stead it gives us back a sense of the potential of each moment, each word, each gesture and each event, and acknowledges the centrality of the processes of creation and expression in all our lives."[8]

The implications of such a poetics lead Duncan to a poetry which, to the conventional eye, seems "unfinished" in its sense of revision, its concept of rime, and its use of what Ezra Pound called "the tone lead-ing of vowels." Rather than revise his work, Duncan reworks the entire poem, treating the first writing as a sketch and subsequent versions as extensions rather than as improvements, with the typing stage com-parable to an orchestration (see, for instance, Cohn and O'Donnell 535). As he says of working on later drafts of *The H. D. Book*, he works "not to correct the original but to live again in its form and content, leaving in successive layers record of reformations and digressions as they come to me" (HD 2.7.53). He seeks not perfection or conclusion but renewal and continuation. "My revisions are my new works, each poem a revision of what has gone before. In-sight. Re-vision. I have learnd to mistrust my judgment upon what I have done. Too often what I thot inadequate proved later richer than I knew; what I thot slavishly derivative proved to be 'mine.'"[9] He has cited Hawthorne's story "The Birthmark" as an example of the dangers of excising a work's "contaminations" (HD 2.8.70–71), and admits that "Often I must force myself to remain responsible to the error that sticks in pride's craw; not to erase it, but to bring it forward, to work with it, even if this flaw mar a hoped-for success" (FC 48). Rhythm and rime, similarly, are considered in new terms, so that rhythm is a matter of time rather than stresses, and the poem's articulations incorporate silence as an essential element. Rime (Duncan's spelling) is taken in the much larger sense of correspondences, the relationships between levels of reality, rather than as merely aural echoes. Sound is pervasively important, the lesson of "the tone leading of vowels," but in ways too subtle for definitive analysis and in fact too various as well: "The vowels are notes of a scale, in which breaths move, but these soundings of spirit upon which the form of the poem depends are not constant. They are the least lasting sounds in our language; even in my lifetime, the sound of my vowels alters. There is no strict vowel standard" (FC 50). Duncan's care for inaccuracies, his pursuit of mistakes, his very sense of the evolutionary growth of a poem, derive from his Whiteheadian notion of the universe, and necessarily contend against the standards of conventional art.

Organic art, he argues, "rises from a deep belief in the universe as a medium of forms, in man's quest as a spiritual evolution. In contrast, conventional art, with its conviction that form means adherence to an imposed order where metric and rime are means of conformation, rises from a belief that man by artifice must win his forms . . . against his nature, areas of control in a universe that is a matter of chaos" (HD Day Book 6). Because Duncan's universe is ultimately and inescapably teleological, he can and even must follow his art where it leads. He condemns systematic rime as he does systematic thought, "for it was careless of the variety of what was actually going on, the lead one sensed in incident, in factors so immediate they seemed chance or accident to all but the formal eye" (HD 2.2.32). By adeptly reversing the charge of carelessness to the conventional art and donning the term *formal,* Duncan argues convincingly for his poetry of the immediate moment.

Articulating his concept of form, Duncan's analogies for "the restless ordering of our poetry" (BB x) are too numerous for all to be examined here: collage, loom, chrestomathy, field, vortex, dance, mosaic, and for a particular example, mobile: "The artist . . . works with all parts of the poem as *polysemous,* taking each thing of the composition as generative of meaning, a response to and a contribution to the building form . . . each part as it is conceived as a member of every other part, having, as in a mobile, an interchange of roles, by the creation of forms within forms as we remember" (BB ix). In a letter, Duncan called attention to Siegfried Giedion's *Mechanization Takes Command*: "A motor, a draft of air, or a push of the hand, will change the state of equilibrium and the interrelations of his suspended elements, connected in a mobile wire system, forming unpredictable, ever-changing constellations and so imparting to them the aspect of space-time." Duncan maintains, "I become more and more concernd with articulation of moving parts, with configurations and constellations in movement—it's interrelationships thruout that I value in working."[10] "Passages," "Structures of Rime," and finally all of Duncan's poetry is not to be read only linearly, but can be rearranged, much as a mobile forms and reforms new shapes unpredictably.

Every poem in *Bending the Bow,* then, is related to every other poem, and to all of Duncan's work. This is true of any good poet's work, of course, but here with a difference, the most striking instance being the intersection of poems. "Structure of Rime XXVI" and "An Illustration: Passages 20" are the same poem (BB 68); the fourth of the five sections of "Apprehensions" is also "Structure of Rime XIV" (RB 39); "Passages 36" is also the eighth of ten poems in "A Seventeenth Century Suite" (GW 80–83). Thus Duncan accentuates the interrelationships of his poetry and emphasizes its mobility.

Duncan developed the constellation analogy in his letter to explain such intersections: "Just as a star which is an element in the configuration of Orion may belong to a galaxy-order far different from any other star in that constellation; and in turn belong to an order of 'star'—so I think of a section-part of the constellation 'Apprehensions' belonging also to another figure 'The Structure of Rime' (here we have co-existence of figures)." Duncan's drawing appears on the facing page. The various levels at which a particular entity can function in Duncan's poetry correspond with the various levels of experiencing reality described by Whitehead. We perceive "Passages 20" as a poem in itself and as part of the "Passages" set, but also as part of "The Structure of Rime," as part of *Bending the Bow,* and as part of Duncan's entire work. In Whitehead's words, "Thus the continuum is present in each actual entity, and each actual entity pervades the continuum" (PR 83).

The permanently open-ended or unfinished poem has ethical implications in that it invites the reader to think of the poet as God. Duncan likens (but does not identify) the artist's creative act to God's (e.g., FC

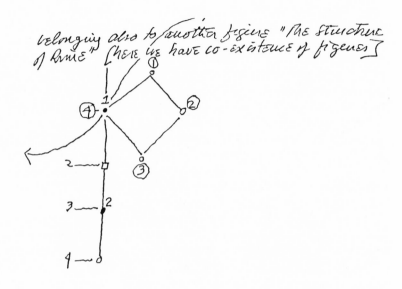

belonging also to another figure "THE structure of Rime" [HERE we have co-existence of figures]

57). Viewing the poet as a quasi-religious figure raises the ultimate possibility that he can achieve perfection, not in the sense of flawlessness but in the etymological sense of *perficere,* to carry through to a finish, to complete. Hence we are again at the crux of a poetics and a cosmology, in an emphasis on process that discounts finality as a delusion. We are confronted with an apparent paradox in the issue of perfection-completion as an attribute of God as opposed to the godlike poet who eschews completeness. But the cosmology apprehended by Whitehead and Duncan dissolves the paradox in its insistence on nonseriality, the processual nature of reality, and the consequent *ongoing* realization of pattern in the world. Duncan's poetry is perfecting rather than perfected. Whitehead's explanation of the dipolar nature of God rejects traditional "notions of a static God condescending to the world, and of a world *either* thoroughly fluent, *or* accidentally static, but finally fluent," recognizing a "double problem: actuality with permanence, requiring permanence as its completion. . . . Either side can only be explained in terms of the other" (PR 409). The view of God

as "completed by the individual, fluent satisfactions of finite fact, and
the temporal occasions . . . completed by their everlasting union with
their transformed selves" (PR 410), requires a new art as well as a new
sense of "perfection."

Duncan never apologizes for the large metaphysical claims he makes
for poetry, nor should he. We are still learning how to read such a
poetry, however, and at times we can be misled by the attractions of
logic and symmetry, as in this passage from Barbara Herrnstein Smith's
study of closure: "Whereas the epigrammatic conclusion will convey
authority, secure conviction, emotional containment, and brusque dis-
missal, the open-ended or anti-closural conclusion will convey doubt,
tentativeness, an inability or refusal to make absolute and unqualified
assertions. It will affirm its own irresolution and compel the reader to
participate in it. As the description suggests, the expressive qualities
of anti-closure, like those of epigrammatic closure, may imply moral
and epistemological attitudes that reach beyond the specific concerns
of the poem. They ask, 'What do we know? How can we be sure we
know it?' They question the validity and even the possibility of unas-
sailable verities, the moral or intellectual legitimacy of final words."[11]
While such efforts can be found in contemporary poetry, they do not
exhaust the possibilities of open poetry. Duncan's art, while question-
ing many moral and epistemological assumptions, nevertheless is not
an art of irresolution but rather the opposite. We should not confuse
the poet's recognition of the ineffability of truth with irresolution. His
is an Emersonian art, hardly irresolute but still demanding the reader's
participation for its full realization. For the process of the poem to
remain fluid, the "final word" must never be spoken; each reader, in
each reading, must enter the field of the poem, experiencing for him
or herself the "impulse toward pattern" (FC 7).

Duncan's response to a direct question about perfection consistently
demonstrated a broader than usual sense of the meaning of the term:
"Perfection, like formulation and formation, can mean either a process
or mean a teleology."[12] The poet's duty is to be prepared for the moment of inspiration, which is not a matter of chance. What is at stake
here is a poetry of a different kind of truth, a different cosmology from
that with which we have traditionally approached not only poetry but
morals and epistemology. That such a view can be intellectually re-
spectable without being logical is attested to by Whitehead: "Each
actuality has its present life and its immediate passage into novelty;

but its passage is not its death. This final phase of passage in God's nature is ever enlarging itself. . . . Thus the universe is to be conceived as attaining the active self-expression of its own variety of opposites—of its own freedom and its own necessity, of its own multiplicity and its own unity, of its own imperfection and its own perfection. All the 'opposites' are elements in the nature of things, and are incorrigibly there. The concept of 'God' is the way in which we understand this incredible fact—that what cannot be, yet is" (PR 412). Duncan's cosmology forbids that perfection of form demanded by traditional ideas of art, truth, and meaning. He accepts that the field of meanings cannot be realized in poetry because "the actual realized poem is just the one form that it is" (FC 51). The field can only be suggested by a small field, set up among various poems or various parts of poems. While reality is process, no single poet occupies the total area of process. The difficulty of recognizing such a paradoxical view of poetry makes that recognition no less necessary if we are to come to a sense of the poetry and its use for us.

Not that Duncan's ideas are exactly new. He often calls himself a derivative poet and is quite explicit about his literary and philosophical lineage. If we find the relationship of poet to spirit unsettling, perhaps we find his ancestors less so only because they are comfortably remote. Emerson aroused fury among conventional men of letters and religion, and today Duncan addresses Emerson's concerns for us. Duncan's propositions, like Emerson's, "propose the general character of the universe." Duncan echoes Emerson's challenge to build our own worlds in a poetry whose thought is prior to its form: "Back of each poet's concept of the poem is his concept of the meaning of form itself; and his concept of form in turn where it is serious at all arises from his concept of the nature of the universe. . . . A mystic cosmogony gives rise to the little world the poet as creator makes" (FC 16–17). Behind the poet and his little world lies "the 'poet' of a poem," who "forces us as writer or reader to obey a compelling form, the necessities of the poem, so that the poet has a likeness to the dreamer of the dream and to the creator of our living reality; dream, reality, and the poem, seem to be one" (HD 1.5.18).

This "'poet' of a poem" is that ultimate designer to whom Emerson built altars and whom Whitehead describes as a God realized only in the process of the world: "God's role is not the combat of productive force with productive force, of destructive force with destructive force;

it lies in the patient operation of the overpowering rationality of his conceptual harmonization. He does not create the world, he saves it; or, more accurately, he is the poet of the world, with tender patience leading it by his vision of truth, beauty, and goodness" (PR 408). Opening himself to the orders of this poet of the world, the human poet enters the field of the poem, granted permission to see what it is and "where it appears." For Duncan, "There is not only the immanence of God, His indwelling, but there is also the imminence of God, His impending occurrence" (FC 81).

God is, then, "what cannot be, yet is," and we are firmly within Duncan's romanticism as "the intellectual adventure of not knowing." Unlike Whitman, who after 1860 became increasingly prophetic, eventually coming to think of himself as more a god than a poet, Duncan, recognizing this "glorious mistake" in his "Poem Beginning with a Line by Pindar," likens the poet to "the creator of the world" without identifying the two. He recognizes in his poetry the "mixed possibilities of inflation and inspiration," noting Dante's frequent need for warnings from Virgil. In this poetry of permission, "the glory is to be universal, not personal. . . . These things, the poet testifies, I did not see by my own virtues, but they were revealed to me" (HD 2.10.61). Acknowledging Whitman's mistaken confusion of poet with prophet, Duncan continues the search of the Pindar poem for the spirit that "restores the land to productive order." The unnumbered Passage, "JA-MAIS," distinguishes between "God's Art, the principle of recognition," and "Man's art, an other arbitration of the whole" (GW 147). While the individual poems of "Passages" or "The Structure of Rime" may appear to be fragments, poet and reader must yield to those forces, to that "impulse toward pattern" of the poet of the world, which will allow them to glimpse the design. The problem of belief is presented at the end of "Passages 32":

> Child of a century more skeptic than
>   unbelieving,   adrift
> between two contrary educations,
> that of the Revolution, which disowns
>   everything,
> and that of the Reaction,
> which pretends to bring back the ensemble
>   of Christian beliefs,

> will I find myself traind to believe
> everything,
>
> as our fathers, the scientists, have been
>
> traind to deny?
>
> (GW 18)

The question of what to believe is ancient, difficult, and crucial. Duncan's poetry is mystical but by no means anti-intellectual. Like the poet, the reader must be prepared for inspiration, must sympathetically attempt to enter the poem. This cosmology offers us not a sense of fragmentation and unknowable truth, but a new hope. Instead of rational structures, a sayable truth, and a static meaning, Duncan offers us participation in the expansive, unfinished process of the poem and of nature, the Emersonian method of "unlocking, at all risks, [our] human doors, and suffering the ethereal tides to roll and circulate through [us]." We do not lose intellect, so much as perceive its place in the process. We do not lose language, but we refuse to "conceive too much of articulation." In the terms of his own description of Whitman, Duncan is "the grand proposer of questions not to be settled, the poet of unsettling propositions," and his poem is "in each phase immediate and complete, but unsatisfied" (FC 164).

The argument from design, even supported by Whitehead's mathematical formulas, will not convince the agnostic, and Duncan refuses to argue:

> no one
>
> nor poet
> nor writer of words
>
> can contrive to do justice to the beauty of that
> design he designs from.
>
> (GW 21)

He is a poet, not a rhetorician, and the poems must be experienced, not explained. But only readers with the strongest preconceptions can remain unmoved by the lyricism and risk and hope of these poems.

Chapter Four

Early Work

Robert Duncan's early work exhibits a wide range of voices, styles—and quality. As with most writers, some of his early poetry embarrassed the mature writer. In the late sixties and early seventies, however, he chose to collect and republish most of it as part of his being the poet that he is. As he states in his introduction to *The Years as Catches*:

What has happened in the almost two decades since *Heavenly City, Earthly City* was written, is that I have come not to resolve or to eliminate any of the old conflicting elements of my work but to imagine them now as contrasts of a field of composition in which I develop an ever-shifting possibility of the poet I am—at once a made up thing and at the same time a depth in which my being is—the poems not ends in themselves but forms arising from the final intention of the whole in which they have their form and in turn giving rise anew to that intention. Poems then are immediate presentations of the intention of the whole, the great poem of all poems, a unity.

(x)

In this remarkably self-perceptive introduction, Duncan acknowledges three poems from 1942—"An African Elegy," "The Years as Catches," and "King Haydn of Miami Beach"—as epitomizing the "disparate strains of my poetry," in which he includes "falseness," "exaggerated pretensions," bloated language, and derivativeness. "But I knew too that the wing of the Adversary, the accusation of falseness and the derivations must be then true to what I was, must be terms in which I must work" (x). Certain poems, then, and particularly the three named above, "have always been clearly recognized as parts of what I have to do in art." He reprints, nonetheless, those poems that continue to embarrass him, suppressing what he elsewhere refers to as "the husk of my modernist pride" in favor of an open recognition, even an active embrace of those disturbances that will continue to inform his art.

Three Key Early Poems

"I don't develop in the sense of growing up. There were only three poems in my earliest work that were indicative of what I was going to have to deal with, and they contradict each other, so I was in 1942 realizing I wasn't going to have any style, observably, at all. . . . The test point would be 'Passages' in which, theoretically, everything can co-exist. It doesn't have any boundaries supposedly. Contradictions are dramatic propositions, and interesting in a poem to get range, to be active throughout" (Mesch 79). These comments, made in a 1974 interview, emphasize the coinherent oneness of Duncan's work. Even as he dismisses his early work and speaks almost disparagingly of his lack of an "observable" style, Duncan links these early poems directly to his most ambitious achievement to date in one grand collage. Later in that same interview he makes the revealing comment: "Heraclitus does not propose dialectics to me. Heraclitus proposes coexistence in a field of contrasting elements" (Mesch 85). That active proposition sets the terms for our understanding of "An African Elegy," "The Years as Catches," and "King Haydn of Miami Beach."

The striking differentness of the three poems testifies to the young poet's testing out various voices and forms. "In this early period I was seeking to find areas of being thru a series of rhetorics—ransacking the theological rhetoric of Milton, the ecstatic rhetoric of Gerard Manley Hopkins, or striving to imitate the demi-surrealist rhetorics of contemporary mannerist poets—Charles Henri Ford, George Barker, or Dylan Thomas" (YAC ii).

An explanation of Duncan's use of the term *rhetoric* is in order here. Fully aware of Ezra Pound's use of the word as a derogatory term and of the word's pejorative connotations in its general use, Duncan characteristically adopts it with some defiance and defines it etymologically as "The flow of speech." Tracing its roots to the Greek word 'ρήτωρ, orator, Duncan observes that the word "had its meaning grounded in the Greek verb *hreo* ('ρέω), to say, that had a pun, at least, if not a root common with the verb *hreo* ('ρέω), to flow. The flow of speech was for the Greeks, as for us, an expression that could refer to words running glibly off a tongue being like a babbling brook and likewise to the speaker's power or fluency. A poet must be fluent in speech; there must be currents of meaning as well as specific meanings" (HD 1.1.19). For Duncan, then, rhetoric is a positive term connoting fluid power of both speech and meaning.

"An African Elegy" (FD 12–14) celebrates the zone of "the marvelous," particularly as it is found in "the mind's / natural jungle." Near
the end of the poem, its metaphor is made all too explicit: "The halls
of Africa we seek in dreams / as barriers of dream against the deep."
The poem nonetheless presents powerful images, such as that of Virginia Woolf, "like a white Afghan hound," responding like Ophelia to
the voice of Death, who "is the dog-headed man zebra striped / and
surrounded by silence who walks like a lion, / who is black." Anticipating *The Venice Poem,* the more important Shakespearean characters
in this poem are Othello and Desdemona, as she "like a demon wails
within our bodies, warns / against this towering Moor of self," while

> in
> jungles of my body, there
> Othello moves, striped black and white,
> the dog-faced fear. Moves I, I, I,
> whom I have seen as black as Orpheus,
> pursued deliriously his sound and drownd
> in hunger's tone, the deepest wilderness.

This delirious pursuit is caught up in the roiling vowels in this passage
and in the ecstatic rhythms of "Negroes, negroes, all those princes,"
lines Duncan's introduction says are derived from Lorca's *Oda al Rey de
Harlem* and other poems.

"The Years as Catches," on the other hand, "caught up, in the midst
of my adoration as a reader of Pound's poetics, my being carried away
as a writer by a Miltonic persuasion" (YAC ii). While Duncan's humor
can mitigate such jarringly contradictory derivations (he told one audience that perhaps Eliot and Pound disliked Milton because they
thought the name was Jewish), his explanation of this title clarifies his
early awareness of the eclectic, inclusive nature of his art: "It is a title
that haunts me still today for it seems to me that my art is indeed such
a net of catches, at once a fishing around for what I can catch and what
catches me at work, and at the same time a fishing by means of such
catches, a music *'writ by catches, with many intervals,'* as the O.E.D.
quotes from Locke, or *'for each succeeding singer to take up or catch his part
in time'"* (YAC ii). Milton and Hopkins succeed Lorca, and are in turn
succeeded by Stevens and Riding in "King Haydn of Miami Beach" as
the three poems together manifest central elements of Duncan's continuing poetic assignment.

The archaic diction and explicit allusions to Milton are followed by the alliterative lines and sprung rhythms of Hopkins as "The Years as Catches" dances its own "interim eternity" between harmony and chaos, but one "that yet shall not avail against the still / unbroken universe of God." Hamilton and Mary Tyler's thoughtful perception about Duncan's "non-belief" sets the context: "The mixture of Neo-Platonic and occult thought of the seventeenth century writers was both a justification for his own heritage and a bridge to its re-examination. It is probably important to his later work that Duncan, because of his theosophical home background, was never quite within the Christian framework and for that reason his non-belief was without the emotional charge of those who have rejected a Christian or Jewish heritage."[1] Like these two unlikely and dissimilar religious poets, a Puritan and a Jesuit, Duncan moves inevitably from Milton's "weary stretch of Christendom" to the godless modern world, "set adrift in the eclipse," from "His harmony, my Chaos" to "my Harmony, His chaos" and finally to an ecstatic breakthrough reminiscent of Hopkins in tone, of Milton in humility, and of both in faith:

> Catch from the years the line of joy,
> impatient & repeated day,
> my heart, break. Eye
> break open and set free
> His world, my ecstasy.
>
> (FD 17)

Regular rhymes and childlike rhythms in "King Haydn of Miami Beach" present yet another very different poem, calling to mind nursery rhymes and, Duncan's introduction alerts us, Laura Riding's *Collected Poems*. He calls her "foster mother to *King Haydn* and *Lovewise*" whose "scolding [of] poets seems, even today, most to be scolding the poet I know myself to be, scolding my very thinking to know and presuming to be" (YAC ix). The portentous tone that clashes with the childlike diction, the oddly named persons of the poem (Mr. Responsible Person, Mr. Do Why, King Haydn), and the juggling of verbs as nouns ("King Haydn abandons the dance of his do") call to mind, of course, Wallace Stevens and E. E. Cummings as well.

The difference of these three key poems indicates something more significant than a simple trying out of various voices by a youthful poet. The ability to don any poetic style remains today for Duncan a virtue (etymologically from *virtu*, a power), empowering him as a poet and generating the creative tensions that produce his multifaceted poetry. In the opening words of the 1966 Introduction to *The Years as Catches,* "These are poems of an irregularity. From the beginning I had sought not the poem as a discipline or paradigm of my thought and feeling but as a source of feeling and thought, following the movement of an inner impulse and tension rising in the flow of returning vowel sounds and in measuring stresses that formed phrases of a music for me, having to do with mounting waves of feeling and yet incorporating an inner opposition or reproof of such feeling." Notable here is his idea of the poem as the source of his thought and feeling rather than the other way around, with the emphasis on the process of the poem's coming into being rather than on the poem as a finished product. That process in turn is informed by the tension of the interplay of opposites, creating not a dialectic but a field of activity in which contrasting elements coexist, not always peacefully.

Duncan's remarkably candid recognition of the shortcomings of the early poetry is rooted in his high expectations of his art and in its risk-taking. As he told Cohn and O'Donnell, a poem presents "an opening in language," but one that "is also an opening into perilous difficulties which you don't quite feel at first. My poems are all hopelessly inadequate. My early poems, of course, are in every occasion hopelessly inadequate" (547).[2] Though harsh, such a verdict is borne out by the stilted rhythms and artificial syntax of "From Richard Burton's *Anatomy of Melancholy*" (YAC 23–24) and by the contrast between the increasingly skillful use of sound and rhythm with the obvious symbolic motifs of "The End of a Year" (58–63). Some notable poems, nonetheless, include the demonic "An Encounter" (21–22) with a darkly abstract double for whom "any stranger is dangerous" and who "tries to define / . . . what art should be or should have been— / wanting it limited, held in the hand against happening"; the oddly optimistic "Homage and Lament for Ezra Pound" (51–53), in which the "old man, early / devoted voice" now "stumbles, mutters maledictions" and for whom spring, "as still as everness returning" offers the apprehension of the permanence of change; and "A Congregation" (65), which sounds early poetic concerns of field, order, disorder, and fragmentation.

Heavenly City, Earthly City

Of all these early poems, *Heavenly City, Earthly City* caused Duncan the most acute embarrassment. As he confessed to Bowering and Hogg, "I had quite a bit of shame about *Heavenly City, Earthly City* and I couldn't read it aloud any longer, and I never republished it until I came to admit, and admitting was not only admitting, it was seeing, yes, this is part of the whole." He then immediately noted the continuing presence of that part of the whole when he said, "So that I guess in *Roots and Branches* you have a returning to a rhetoric of earlier form" (n.p.). A young poet, admirer of Pound, Joyce, and other modernists, might well be embarrassed by this poem's elegiac rhetoric, by its posturing defiance in the face of "the clamor of a dismal century," by its speaker's unconvincing identification with Icarus and Orpheus and his equally unconvincing assertions (e.g., "There is no world other than the world of my dreams"), and by its bald apostrophe to the "Turbulent Pacific" as an "Insistent questioner of our shores! / Somnambulist! old comforter!" "I drift, I drift," the poem tells us, and one can only agree. The presence of "Returning to a Rhetoric of an Earlier Mode" in *Roots and Branches* must have been an agonizing admission, yet a necessary recognition that many of the themes and devices of *Heavenly City, Earthly City* remain active in Duncan's work as a fully accepted "geist of rhapsodic excess in a time / despising the rush, the being carried away" (RB 90).

Medieval Scenes

The First Decade juxtaposes two starkly different groups of poems from 1947, *Domestic Scenes* and *Medieval Scenes*. Duncan has said he wrote the first in homage to William Carlos Williams, and their titles would seem congenial to Williams's maxim, "No ideas but in things": "Breakfast," "Bus Fare," "Mail Boxes," "Electric Iron," "Lunch with Buns," and so forth. Duncan at this time could no more write in Williams's manner than he could fly, of course, and one can only imagine Williams's reaction to this stanza from "Radio":

> But take this swindle of the heart,
> I love you. There is a swank
> of realistic swans, moon-certain birds,
> truthful joys in that dishonest swamp,
> painted lugubriousness of Hollywood lagoon.
>   (FD 48)

According to Duncan, Williams responded with "a blast" that "there was no American language in there." He could laugh about it in his 1969 interview with Bowering and Hogg: "Of course I have never

written in American language, nor did I ever in my whole life. But
that letter was in itself an inspiration, because then with vengeance I
wrote *Medieval Scenes*" (n.p.).

The serial poem *Medieval Scenes* was Duncan's first strong long poem,
one he called "my suite of heresies" (HD 2.9.45). While his interest
in medieval and Renaissance studies would lead him back to Berkeley
and the scholar Ernst Kantorowicz, Duncan is careful to note that the
poem was written a year before that, and while he and his circle talked
of medieval romances and mysteries, "there is no medieval learning in
the poem beyond the childhood stories and lore shared by all of us who
loved tales of wonder and enchantment. *Medieval Scenes* is curious, not
learned; written in a certain valuable glow of imagining the world of
the poem untainted by such knowledge as might have raised questions
of belief or disbelief" (n.p.). He further recalls, in his preface to *Medieval Scenes 1950 and 1959,* that the poem was not composed but
performed "to exhibit mediumistic powers as well as to reach the voice
of an oracle beyond." The poem was written on ten consecutive nights
in February, 1947. Robert Bertholf's afterword to *Medieval Scenes 1950
and 1959* carefully describes the procedure of the writing and the complex history of its revisions and publication. Bertholf observes of Duncan's early poems that he "initiated himself into an order of poetry in
which the generation of form, as opposed to adherence to convention,
claimed first importance." Bertholf also cites the "Author's Notes" to
the poems, in which Duncan acknowledges that in this book he "had
the sense for the first time in poetry not just of 'having' a poem, being
seized by this utterance that had to fulfill itself, but of having a work
to do and knowing that work as I did it."

The poems project a fantastic world, peopled with figures and persons like those that emerge more powerfully in later work such as "The
Structure of Rime." Duncan here also interrogates the nature of poetry
and of inspiration, with several meditations on the Muse's power—
both imaginative and sexual—over the poet, who is seen as a "bearish
magicker" and an "unawakened dreamer." He asks in "The Festivals"
(1950), "Was it a dream, or was it memory?" A condescending poet
regards "his foolish Muse" and tells himself, "The sleeping joy / . . .
is best." His phrase is interrupted, however, by the words, "he mur-
murs in her dream," and the ominous hum of the sounds warns us of
the poet's folly. In one of a number of places in the sequence that alert
us that Williams is much on Duncan's mind, the poet dismisses "Our
unicorn" as "but a gilded ass." The Muse insists, "You are a wondrous

sleeping / in a world of wonders. . . . I saw [the braying ass] in my dream and dreamt / he was a magic wonder." The terrors of inspiration come home in the poem's final lines, "The Muse, amused, / awakens the fearful poet to her dream."

The fearfulness derives from the possession involved in both love and poetic inspiration, a loss of self that Duncan refuses to gloss over as transcendence. In both versions, "The Albigenses," the final poem of the series, asserts:

> The spirits of the Light move in the dark.
> They strive to touch. We know
> dim memories of their chastity.
>
> I know a serpent wisdom of the blood,
> of suffering, of coital magic.
> The light of our spirit is draind away
> into the flesh.

And a few lines later,

> The poet lovers in copulation know
> the emergence of the dragon from all things.
> They burn in the wrath of the wrathful God.
> Black is the beauty of the brightest day.
>
> *O let me die, but if you love me, let me die.*
> *Your grief and fury hurt my second life.*

Sex and poetry alike present competing claims on one's energies, and both provide for the apprehension—a fearful knowing, to pick up both senses of the word—which informs Duncan's later work and poetics. One key to this series, then, is the punning of "mere" and "more" which Duncan added to four of the poems as he prepared a reading version (see Bertholf's afterword), perhaps most concisely glossed by Duncan himself in "Figures of Speech" in *Letters*: "It is thru language that we can imagine the universe. How shall we explain that seeing, touching, smelling, hearing, are all mere and that desire moves us toward more—and the imagination is of this more" (D 103–04). With this series, Duncan felt "seized by this utterance that had to fulfill itself," and he comments in his preface, "I came upon the mode in

which the eternal ones of the poem might come to speak to me . . . ,
where I consulted with fates that still stand over my work today"
(n.p.). As Bertholf states in his afterword, then, "The series stands as
an elegant gate between the early and late poetry."

The Venice Poem

Whereas in writing *Medieval Scenes* Duncan knew what must be
done, "what the poem wanted," *The Venice Poem* was the first poem in
which he not only knew what must be done "but also how to do it.
. . . In *The Venice Poem,* the world of the poem was not a scene received
and rendered [as it had been in *Medieval Scenes*] but a matrix, within
which and through which I lived, into which I brought my actual life,
the unfortunate course of love and betrayal which I suffered during the
time of writing, not in order to express what I experienced but in order
to take what I experienced as a passion, to in-form myself with the
content of the poem" (HD 2.7.67). Duncan's first unquestionable master work, *The Venice Poem* manifests the key elements of the poetics of
Duncan's later work: multiple derivations; attention to melos, following the lead of sounds toward an open invention or discovery; and
consequently, permitting the poem to unfold itself from the rimes of
sound and image, generating itself out of apparently incidental experiences and memories into the realization of a larger picture.

All these elements come together in this poem's use of the other
arts—specifically music, painting, architecture, sculpture, drama, and
film—for both structural analogues and thematic leads or rimes. The
poem's two primary derivations are Jane Harrison's *Themis* and Igor
Stravinsky's *Symphony in Three Movements.* (More explicit allusions to
Othello, Lorenzo Bernini, Henri Rousseau, and William Blake are in-
cremental and thematic rather than structurally significant.) The musical nature of both is of paramount importance to the poem, itself
structured as a three-part sonata with coda. Duncan called to Jonathan
Williams's attention Harrison's importance to *The Venice Poem* in an
undated letter now in the archives at SUNY-Buffalo: "All of Chapter
II of THEMIS is vital to seeing the primitive concept of the VENICE
POEM."[3] Noting that the poem is "a construction of movements
within a given area of time; propositions of areas; movements of and
countermovements to ideas," Duncan concentrates on Harrison's discussion of the dithyramb as "a form of lyric, full of thrill in its very

name, but excited, exotic, apt to become licentious." The choric danc-
ers, Duncan is careful to note, emphasize the collective emotion and
sink their personal identities "by the wearing of masks and disguises,
by dancing to a common rhythm, above all by the common excitement, they become emotionally one, a true congregation."[4] Evident
here is Duncan's growing awareness of the projective powers of poetry—Harrison describes even the projection of "the raw material of
god-head" in dithyrambic ritual—and of its communal nature. As a
consequence, here and in his later poetry he uses such "masks and
disguises" and emphasizes generation of hypnagogic states through the
dance of image and sound.

Duncan's letter to Williams also calls attention to *The Venice Poem*'s
"musical composition in three movements (each movement having an
advancing tide and returning tide)." He speaks elsewhere of the "or-
chestrations" of the poem, "for I was following impulses towards design that haunted me in listening to the *Danses Concertantes* and the
Symphony in Three Movements of Stravinsky where it seemed to me that
form impended thruout, that every particular of the structure was
charged by the numen of the whole." While he uses Stravinsky's general structure, he disarmingly goes on to admit, "having no musical
literacy, certainly having only an analogical understanding, I derived
certainties of my own aesthetic, and then of a poetic, of a theory of
forms and of the nature of making itself, as I have derived understandings from sciences I do not 'really understand'" (HD 2.7.55). This
comment throws valuable light on Duncan's use of his "derivations" as
well as on the structure of *The Venice Poem,* and the poem is indeed a
crucial advance in his theory of forms.

Symphony in Three Movements is the product of Stravinsky's "classical
period" of about 1920–50, which caused much resentment among
avant-garde musicians because of its references to older styles. Stravinsky, like Duncan, recognized that an artist builds on the work of others, that innovators must also be rooted in tradition. The complex form
of the sonata typically consists of exposition, development, recapitu-
lation, and coda (Stravinsky's symphony lacks the coda), with the
movements having an overall unity of subject and style but differing
in tempo, rhythm, and melody. *The Venice Poem* is structured as a three-
part sonata with coda, and its movements also differ in pace, rhythm,
and tone. Duncan appropriates Stravinsky's aural excitement and har-
monic dynamism, his use of patterns of rhythmic tension calculated in

terms of time units, the interplay of loudness and softness, motion and rest, repetition and nonrepetition, weighed against each other as the piece progresses. Duncan is hardly musically illiterate, and his "analogical understanding" enabled him to adapt the form to his poem in ways strikingly parallel to Stravinsky's symphony, the first section *allegro,* the second *andante,* and the third *con moto.* In fact, when Ezra Pound wrote to Duncan that the poem "should have had a plan," Duncan's rueful recognition was "that the work had been circumscribed by its schematic design" ("Notes on Grossinger's *Solar Journal,"* n.p.).

Not only the symphony but Stravinsky's *Poetics of Music* influenced the poem's conception. Stravinsky's book emphasized poetics as "the study of work to be done," and it clarified Duncan's idea of melody. From Stravinsky's definition, "melody, *Mélôdia* in Greek, is the intonation of the *melos,* which signifies a fragment, a part of a phrase," Duncan reports that "that year, working on the Venice Poem, I had begun to follow the lead of the immediate particular towards an open invention. 'Watch the duration of syllables, the tone leading of vowels,' Pound had instructed" (HD 2.2.31–32). Stravinsky and Pound together led Duncan to the melodic breakthrough of *The Venice Poem.*

The poem opens with "A Description of Venice," specifically La Piazza San Marco, dominated by the Basilica and also bordered by the Doge's Palace. Venice, then, calls to mind the square and its lion statues, the cathedral's bells, its four bronze horses and winged lion, and the canals, but also Shakespeare's *Othello.* Into this matrix, Duncan brought his "actual life, the unfortunate course of love and betrayal" cited earlier, and these elements together in-form, give form to, the poem as it proceeds and as its allusions proliferate. The poem's intermingling of dream and vision with cold hard fact serves to make one wary of easy generalizations. Like Othello, the poet is "tortured with voices" and curses time itself, measured in the bells' ringing, "Damn the persistent tolling of the hour." Time itself, he says, turns the blue of sky and water "to watery green," as jealous rage infects all. Desdemona is not "mere spirit but body," another "perishable beauty / of imperishable Venice" (85).

The second half of the first movement, "Testimony," carries us back to the poem's opening lines and begins the specific articulation of the poem's poetics:

> "These natural sounds suggest music,
>   but are not yet themselves music."

When they seemingly arrange themselves,
    so subtly the traind mind arranges,
then there appears from the swift fingers writing
    what the ear hears; word and vision
seem inspiration. As if the goddess herself,
    awful and lovely, spoke to the dumb poet
more than he knew.

                                                    (86)

At this point the poem rapidly begins to unfold its many possibilities. The "jewel blue eyes" of the "bronze boy" from the opening lines, then "a central sapphire, / cruel and absolute" (81), becomes "My jealousy is like a jewel, a sapphire / or sapphire needle, 'good for 1000 performances,' / cruel and absolute, from which comes my music" (87). The stinging, sharp needle of jealousy generates the poem, like the phonograph needle which is presumably playing Stravinsky. "Great Jealousy herself" is recognized as one of the many "avatars" or incarnations of "Our Lady Love," whose "many / individual perfections . . ."

        strike a music in the blood, a melody
    "scattered to the winds with indefatigable profusion,"
        which, set into order, emerges
    as the central portion, the symphonic *allegro*,
        jeweld perfection of music's hierarchy.

                                                    (87)

Not only having returned to the first section as Stravinsky's symphony does, but also having specifically underlined its own *allegro* quality, the first movement concludes, "There is no pain / that I would not bear for her sake." The interwoven ecstasies and agonies of love and art will continue to inform this poem.

The *andante* second movement, "Imaginary Instructions," presents "another world . . . / beyond my hand," phrasing that echoes Duncan's description of deriving understandings he does not "really understand" from Stravinsky and also the communal excitement of the dithyramb. Acknowledging that "the individual man is self-central," the poem directly addresses inflation, the turned head, as a primary danger of this poetry:

        Sometimes the diadems of poetry
            —mock gold glories cut out from paper

> of an afternoon—
>   turn until my head turns, inflate
> a bulbous image of a world, a vulgar empire.
> And I can sit upon a throne,
>   cross-eyed king of one thousand lines.
> In the mirror of poetry I conjure
>   luxuries I can ill afford.
>   (88)

Like a superstitious young girl seeking the image of her future lover on St. Agnes Eve, the poet can delude himself with the "many faces, forms, glances / the phantom lover had," again recalling the many faces of Our Lady Love from part one.

Suddenly Lorenzo Bernini's famous bust of Louis XIV enters the poem, described in accurate detail. "Why does it come to mind / now?" the poet asks himself. "Why are we never at rest, I ask. / Why am I toucht so deeply?" (89). The question immediately evokes again the "root" of this poetic, the faith and trust required of both poet and lover.

> There is a root, faithless and painful,
>   from which we spring.
>   Why does the rose
>   never cease unfolding
>   but grows and unfurls—
> the swirl, the twist,
>   the savage despair of draperies
>   so that its beauty
>   surpasses knowing?
>   (89)

A terrifying vortex opens up in the poem, imaged in the rose (used in similar ways by Hart Crane in "Voyages") and in "the savage despair" of the draperies of Bernini's bust of the king, and the poem presents its shocking self-recognition:

> —This is not the exalted face
>   Bernini saw—
> the forlorn cocksucker is not wonderful.
>   (89)

In such a "humiliating moment," the poet asserts, "Only passion can rise to the occasion." Duncan's punning sense of humor should never be entirely forgotten. Nonetheless, the continuing thematic link of sex and poetry sets up the poem's concluding parallel losses, the lover's betrayal begetting a corresponding loss of faith in poetry. Here in the second movement, dreamers are dismissed as "lotophagoi," the indolent, dreamy lotus eaters. Even so, the poem insists, "Yet here seeks the heart solace," even in the homosexual love which "Nature barely provides for."

And here, of all places, Duncan cites Pound's advice about attending to "what is happening," to "'the duration of syllables, / 'the melodic coherence, / 'the tone leading of vowels' / 'The function of poetry is to debunk by lucidity'" (91). Even as the poem's light quite literally exposes all pretensions, the poem's very syllables, *melos*, vowels generate "How many faces, forms . . . / each, as if omnipotent. / / This is Love. Our Lady / appears and reappears" (91). Thus alerted, the attentive reader turns and returns with a new eye to passages of the poem that are, like Bernini's bust of "the inventing head," both *"vif et brilliant"* (92).

The poem's opening lines, for instance, present lions—with always an aural pun on lines, as in a poem—echoed in the key word *suppliant*, and another diphthong leading the ear in *crouch, tower,* and *sound.* Alliteration and the long *u* intensify the line, "the bronze boy burns the blue sky / with jewel blue eyes." As important to the passage's effect are the *differences* of vowel sounds that depend on their full context for their effect. The syllables, we realize, led to the plays on *holy, hail,* and *heal* (82), *Venice* and *Venus* (83), *heart* and *hurt* (84), and so on, until the apprehension causes apprehensiveness, threatens to overwhelm.

Yet more. Leap ahead to the poem's climactic passage (98–100), its insistence on "first forms," a remarkable crescendo of allusion, sound, and theme as we are asked to listen to Henri Rousseau's painting *The Dream.* The various arts merge, in a poem about a painting that is musical. Again, the passage reminds us explicitly to attend to "the tone leading of vowels, / in the humming, the hesitating" (99). The poem pushes its frustrations—both in love and in art—to the literal limits, crystallizing in a description of the coming into being of the poem itself at the edge of dream and reality:

Henri Rousseau, *The Dream* (1910). Museum of Modern Art, New York City. "The image lifts into gesture / like the hand pointing / or the trunk lifting / or the silent black man / holding the pipe as a gesture . . ." (*The Venice Poem*).

> This is the painter's real world.
> She hesitates upon the verge of sound.
> She waits upon a sounding impossibility,
>   upon the edge of poetry.

>   (99)

"The image lifts into gesture," the poem continues, and the gesture lifts into "the throat pulsating / into the duration of syllables." The poem's coherence is only in its melody, its fragments, which coalesce in the vision of Venus rising out of the sea, an impossible transformation of chaos into Beauty.

> She rose out of a great rustling of waters,
> transformd in the sea roar
> within the shell.

What is happening?

music, magic,
emerging

out of the shell-coil ear

the mimic murmur,
the remembering.

(100)

"We must understand what is happening," Pound had instructed, and the question here emphasizes that such understanding comes not through logic but through trust, faithfully following the poem's "impulses toward design" to such a "sounding impossibility."

Part three, "The Venus of Lespuges," returns to the motifs of the first movement. "I return to first things" (96), this time in the paleolithic image of Venus, which the poem again relates to music as the head and "violin neck / above the female musical body / seem instrumental, / the deep strings of the viol / waiting for sound." An apparent disruption by two Greek words only reinforces the theme. The first, Ἀφροδίτη, names Aphrodite, the Greek equivalent of Venus, and the second, μῆτερ, links *mater,* mother, with *meter,* measure, and thus fertile sexuality with poetry. The next turn presents her as "the queen of hearts / above the ace of spades, / the creator or destroyer" now seen as wearing the mask of Eleanor of Aquitane (herself both politically adept and a patroness of the arts) as well as of Rousseau's "Mistress of the tiger." In her many guises, she both unifies and confounds. "She has such art, / confounding all things . . . / / the weight of her breasts, / the weight of her words" (97; Duncan's ellipses). In yet another appropriate pun, this art confounds in several senses. Just as meter and measure, sexuality and art and, in the immediately following pages, music and magic, all merge, this art mixes together, but it also bewilders, even embarrasses. Despite its schematic structure, *The Venice Poem* foreshadows Duncan's later art of the conglomerate or collage.

The interplay of opposites, not in dialectical resolution but coexisting in a field whose very tensions generate the art, informs Stravinsky's *Symphony in Three Movements,* Duncan's *Venice Poem,* and most of Duncan's work since then. Whatever artistic metaphor Duncan uses to describe his "analogical understanding" of art, he insists on following

those "impulses toward design" wherever they lead. When the music
and magic merge, even in the most disturbing apprehensions, then the
faith and trust of both poet and reader are rewarded.

Caesar's Gate

Duncan collected a series of poems from 1949 to 1950 along with
some "paste-ups" by Jess under the title *Caesar's Gate*. First published
as a book in 1955, it appeared with some prose poems written in that
year to illustrate some of the paste-ups. The book was reissued in 1972
with a new preface, epilogue, and an added poem, "Despair in Being
Tedious," which also appears in *Ground Work, Volume One.* Here again
are poems Duncan continues to find humiliating, as he told Abbott
and Shurin, for the book is filled with "a tremendous rage and desolation" at his being left by a lover (*Sunshine* 5). Duncan titles one group
of poems "Poetic Disturbances," extending the mode of *The Venice Poem*
with thematic and structural interruptions. To this date, he continues
to use digressions and interruptions in order to disrupt his poems and
keep them open to contingency. As interesting as the poems, however,
are the preface and epilogue added in 1972. The preface admits most
of the poems are "poetically questionable," but skillfully responds to
the criticisms of M. L. Rosenthal that his poetry is sentimental.[5] It
also contains insights into the "imperialism" of *The Venice Poem* and the
gradual movement of his later poetry toward *The Opening of the Field.*
Indeed, because "it proposes a dissatisfaction that belongs to my present work as I know it," Duncan admits, "I am not done then with
Caesar's Gate" (xxxvi). The epilogue is similarly valuable, an extended
recounting of a hypnagogic state, moving in "The Matter of the Bees"
from its recognition that "Myths are the dream data of history" (62) to
a fascinating swarm of idea, allusions, and associations. Duncan follows
his "hypnagogic phantasy" across a field of eclectic memories, so that
as the preface began by admonishing Rosenthal's refusal to follow his
feeling, the book concludes with Duncan following his.

Duncan closed *First Decade* appropriately with "Song of the Border-
guard." With its incessant puns on *lion* and *line,* the poem presents the
poet on guard, threatened by the poem. "The sound of words waits—
/ a barbarian host at the borderline of sense" (135). The lion of poetry
waits for the poet to let his guard down, waits to possess him. Where
the preface of *Caesar's Gate* warned us that boundaries define what we
abhor as well as what we would be (xxxiv), this poem recognizes that

"the borderlines of sense in the morning light / are naked as a line of poetry in a war." Such an ambivalent view of poetry, of the terror and joy of inspiration, has been fully incorporated into Duncan's work.

Two Plays

Another sign of Duncan's energy in the 1950s is his production of two plays, *Medea at Kolchis: The Maiden Head,* first presented at Black Mountain College on 29 and 30 August 1956, and *Faust Foutu,* presented in a dramatic reading at The Six gallery in San Francisco in January 1955. Both plays use avant-garde techniques, both freely update classical myths in terms of the artist as protagonist, and both present further evidence of Duncan's evolving sense of his art.

Duncan's *Medea* focuses on the young girl's betrayal of her father for the love of Jason rather than on the later episode recounted by Euripedes. Set in 1904, the play presents a young poet, Jason, who is driven by "an old story / that I do not believe nor understand" (18) to betray Arthur Griffith, an older poet whose work he has learned by heart. Arthur possesses the Fleece, now only the sign of enchantment, "a glitter left over where power once moved" (12). Because of his inhuman vision of poetry as "a luminous uncertainty, a great articulation, autonomous, no respecter of person, contradictory and beautiful" (28), Arthur has rejected love and humanity: "The self! the person! . . . I have come to loath all person, because it corrupts, reduces, cripples the man or woman who might have been a magnificent figure" (28). Opposed to him are the intensely physical Jason (who admits, "I am driven / toward that gain that gains me nothing, / driven to take the prize of the universe / before which I know I am unworthy" [17]) and Medea, who at the moment of Arthur's stroke proclaims, "I am grown snake, pregnant with my self" (29). Just as Medea is seized by "unholy certainties," Jason longs for the return of a primitive simplicity, an era before the poets "calld down the gods" and broke all boundaries: "Silence the Fleece and the innocence of life will return" (37). With three other characters who function as both the Fates and a chorus, the play enacts its vision of the fabulous, with its images of trembling flames and flowers notably prefiguring a key motif of *The Opening of the Field.* Despite its radical re-vision of the story, Duncan's play asserts, in Arthur's words, "These ancient things reoccur" (10), or as Duncan's preface states, the play is related less to Greek tragedy than "to the primitive theater of each of us in our own lives. . . . It has seemed to me that all man's psychic and spiritual life arises in such play with physical realities, using his actual body as it uses his actual world about him to enact its drama" (iv).

Even as he had not yet finished *Faust Foutu,* Duncan described it in terms that apply to all his work: "Everywhere dissenting, contradictory voices speak up, I find. I don't seek a synthesis, but a mellee [sic]." In these "Notes Midway on My Faust"[6] he admits to many influences, but not Goethe's *Faust,* which he had not read! More significant, he accurately describes the play's concerns: "The problem is that we dread all inconsequential experience; our taboo is at root against unintelligible passions." The result is a play that is, indeed, "no pleasure for aesthetes. A composite, indecisive literature."

The completed play, as we might expect, is excessively clever, at times impossible to follow, downright silly, pretentious, highly self-reflexive, and a good deal of fun (it is, after all, a play, he reminds us). Its title, a French vulgarism loosely translated as "Faust Fucked," indicates its outrageous sexuality. Its energy is manifest in its incessant punning, its inspired silliness (Faust calls it "inspired ennui," [29]), and its assault on the Korean War and the inverted values of contemporary America by way of the aesthetics of Gertrude Stein and dada. The play circumvents its audience's expectations wherever possible. I.6 is interrupted by III.2, a scene unrelated to the second scene of the third act we see later. In the middle of an apology by "the Author" for "this monstrous design, this play," a member of the audience disrupts the play to end III.2, which indeed appeared to be endless, and the following scene includes a frank discussion of "Robert Duncan's work" ("He's terribly uneven you know"). The fourth act, "a soliloquy for five voices," would be literally unintelligible in performance as the five spoke simultaneously in a "Quintet of Voices."

For all its silliness, the play confronts deep themes and "unintelligible passions." A self-described "bird cackle and boneplay, an anglo-saxon mummery and a keltic dada" (60), *Faust Foutu* is also "a play in which terror was playful" and a treatment of the author's dis-ease, even as he confesses to "the voluptuous joy of throwing my selves away, of spending my energies fruitlessly" (62). As he reports in "Notes Midway on My Faust," "I have 'selected' my works, weeded out the poetry which is not all of a tone, and composed a works that has a remote consistency. But resurrect everything: and one will discover my true book" (2). This chaotic "play ground" was a necessary foreground for the shapely wholeness of *The Opening of the Field.*

Derivations: Selected Poems 1950–1956

Duncan collected most of his other poetry prior to *The Opening of the Field* in *Derivations: Selected Poems 1950–1956.* The book opens with "An Essay at War," which Duncan acknowledges "proposed pretty much the process of my later poetry" (Mesch 80). Its opening lines set the terms forth quite plainly:

> The design of a poem
>   constantly
> under reconstruction,
>   changing, pusht forward;
> alternations of sound, sensations;
>   the mind dance
> wherein thot shows its pattern:
>   a proposition
> in movement.
>
>   (9)

The poem develops its theme of design, both as "a hidden thing / reveald in its pulse and / durations" and as conniving deception, by contrasting the conscious design of dominance then apparent in the hell of the Korean War with the dynamic, processual design of Duncan's poetics. Recoiling from the "terror self-containd" of Tanagra figures and carefully regular Alexandrines, the poem instead aims at imperfection: "The imperfection proposed, studied / in the cloudy stone, claims adoration" (15). In contrast to MacArthur's will to victory, the poem proposes, "Let us resolve / the right surrender" (17). At war, in love, or in poetry, one's designs must constantly undergo reconstruction:

> To fail! To fall? without a plan,
> doesn't everything turn out poorly?
> Sure to surrender to the critic's contempt!
>   (22)

This poem proposes the contrast between military orders and the larger orders of poetry that flowers most fully in *Bending the Bow.*

Appropriate to the title, much of the rest of *Derivations* is given over to Duncan's imitations of Gertrude Stein, skillful and often witty but finally extended finger exercises, such as the plays on "spelling" and "casting a spell" in the series *word, bird, heard, absurd,* and then *hard, ward,* and *bard* (31). Key concepts can be seen here in gestation (e.g., "Motto": "A correspondence is a poetry enlarged," [51]), but this is joyful play as well: "What do we know then but seeking to know the stretch and the shrinking, the sureness of aim and the aimless surety the feeling of security in reciting what we are doing, the fun of pursuing the ensuing phrases" (46). Stein's self-description from *The Autobiography of Alice B. Toklas* describes Duncan's method as well: "She also liked then to set a sentence for herself as a sort of tuning fork and metronome and then write to that time and tune."[7]

Letters: Poems 1953–1956 (1958), however, presents the next poetic breakthrough. As Duncan describes his own development, *Heavenly City, Earthly City, Medieval Scenes,* and *The Venice Poem* had been "forms embodying or expressing the content of an inner psychological drama," whereas with *Letters* Duncan, "already a convert to the Romantic spirit," now saw that "myth in that spirit is not only a story that expresses the soul but a story that awakens the soul to the real persons of its romance, in which the actual and the spiritual are revealed, one in the other" (FC 31).

The letters of the title refer not to any correspondence through the mail but to the letters of the alphabet seen as mysterious signs in themselves, in the tradition of both Jewish and Christian Kabbalists. The Jewish Kabbalists believed the Torah contained the mysteries of the universe, but that they were revealed only through inspired meditation on the letters themselves, which had their own creative powers. As Rodger Kamenetz explains, the *Zohar* "enters into Christian thought through Pico della Mirandola during the Renaissance, and later, in Europe and America, through various theosophical movements. All of this came to Robert Duncan in childhood through the Christian hermeticism of his parents." In this theory of correspondence, "every event at the cosmic level has its counterpart in the mundane" (9).

With such an underpinning of faith, *Letters* proposes "a process of re-vision and disorganization" (90), a rejection of purpose or conscious design in order to allow the cosmic design to emerge. Such "discontinuities of poetry" make possible "the peril of beauty" (91). Duncan knew that such a poetry would be attacked in the 1950s, as he wrote to Jonathan Williams that the book "shld stick in the critical craw: it must so to those wolves of stupidity. Surely it will elicit (illicit) the proper gleeful yelps of scorn. It's so flagrantly exalted and bookish."[8]

In taking apart the very language, Duncan anticipates, playfully,

some of the critical preoccupations that threaten to drown criticism
itself now, thirty years later.

> Why knot ab stract
> a tract of mere sound
> is more a round
> of dis abs cons
>   t r a c t i o n
> —a deconstruction—
> for the reading of words.
> (95)

On the same page, he has fun as well with his own tradition.

> the addition of the un
> plannd for interruption:
> a flavor stinking coffee
> (how to brew another cup
> in that Marianne Moore-
> E.P.-Williams-H.D.-Stein-
> Zukofsky-Stevens-Perse-
> surrealist-dada-staind
> pot)   by yrs R.D.

Such playfulness serves as a background to the necessary change and
renewal that informs his poetics.

"It is thru language that we can imagine the universe. . . . All that
is merely sensible objects to or yields to the urgencies of ours to dream
the world" (103). With such themes, Duncan enters fully into his romantic world, Blake's "full splendor of poetry in which we blindly see"
(103). In 1953, Helen Adam read Blake to a workshop "in a sublime
and visionary manner, as if what was important was not the accom-
plishment of the poem but the wonder of the world of the poem itself,
breaking the husk of my modernist pride and shame, my conviction
that what mattered was the literary or artistic achievement" (FC 30).
With such a breakthrough, Duncan sets forth in his romantic poetry,
an "intellectual adventure of not knowing" (FC 46), less concerned
with his own fame or artfulness and more conscious that "I work at the
language as a spring of water works at the rock, to find a course, and
so, blindly. In this I am not a maker of things, but, if maker, a maker
of a way" (D 130). Only such a poetics can encompass "the recalcitrant

incoherence" (114), can enter into "the immediacy of which I speak, or the coinherence as Charles Williams calld it" (118), and can "partake of / A lamp of letters, a ladder of / divine signs" (120).

Duncan expected such a poetry to baffle the uninitiated and outrage the conventional (those who "scorn the effluvia of mistake, misuse, misunderstanding—the whole spiritualized universe," [137]), but he followed its lead against his own tendency to overcompose, as he told Howard Mesch: "I'd love to have more decomposition, and *Letters,* of course, does propose that; that's the shawl falling apart and the things with holes" (Mesch 85). He put it more memorably in *Letters,* in "An owl is an only bird of poetry": "It is in the disorders of the net that the stars fall from the designs we grasp into their original chaos" (D 132).

This breakthrough led, by way of several intersecting paths, to the open field poetry of Duncan's major poetry. Even science comes to inform this poetics. Duncan had been alerted by Charles Olson to Whitehead's *Process and Reality* by 1957, and was reading Whitehead while writing the poems that would appear in *The Opening of the Field.* Even before that stands Duncan's strict Darwinism: that science's "generative idea . . . is strict, straight-line Darwinism—which is *no purpose.* And there damn well better not be a purpose, because you're lost if there is" (Cohn and O'Donnell 536). Thus *Letters* refers to "the diabolist Pavlov and the spiritualist Einstein" (91). Duncan had the *virtu,* the power, to recognize his insight for what it was, and it led him into his major books of poetry even as he began belittling his own role. "What my life work will be is entirely there at the point when I begin *The Opening of the Field.* You find its content and its propositions are in the preceding period, from 1952 to 1956, and it takes place in the book *Letters*; and from there on I have a work assigned, and it's, as Charles would say, a vector" (Cohn and O'Donnell 525).

Chapter Five
The Opening of the Field (1960)

For readers new to Duncan's work, *The Opening of the Field* is probably his best book to start with. It contains several excellent short lyrics, the widely anthologized Pindar poem, and the first thirteen sections of the continuing sequence "The Structure of Rime." Moreover, it demonstrably succeeds as a *book,* a carefully presented collection whose sum is greater than its parts, and it does so in ways even novice readers can perceive.

The book opens with the poem that establishes the controlling images of field, play, flowers, fire, boundary, and permission, "Often I Am Permitted to Return to a Meadow." Duncan's recurring dream of a reconciled world is evoked in five masterful sentences. That world is his and not his, a made place and an eternal pasture. Paradox is not irony, of course, but rather a circumvention of logical reasoning in an attempt to enter a different way of thinking. That different way of thinking's Platonic roots are revealed when we are told that this made place is "created by light / wherefrom the shadows that are forms fall."

These forms or "architectures" are actually likenesses of "the First Beloved." The field of the poem, which the poet is permitted to enter—often, but not as a matter of his will alone—presents "flowers [which] are flames lit to the Lady." Such an intermixture of flame and flower will recur, or rime, in key passages of the book, and indeed close it, at the end of "Food for Fire, Food for Thought."

What is the significance of flaming flowers? The children's game is "ring a round of roses," the medieval chant to ward off the plague inverted to a game—"ashes, ashes, all fall down." But this metaphor is central in Duncan's poetics: blossoming is followed by decay, destruction inevitably follows upon realization and is superseded in its turn by renewal. Dust returns to dust inevitably, but this is a fertilizing decay from which new life, phoenixlike, arises.

The field is the major figure of the book, proposing the poem as an area of activity rather than as a static object. The poem's movement is spatial, multidirectional rather than linear. The poet enters this poem as a matter of permission, but must be an active participant, prepared for the opportunity. The field, then, is "not mine, but is a made place, / / that is mine." The locus of the field is immaterial, in both senses: it does not matter where the poet (or reader) may physically be, and it is not matter but spirit. Thus the Platonic overtones of the field's being "created by light / wherefrom the shadows that are forms fall."

In an act of faith ("as if"), the poet accepts as a "given property of the mind / that certain bounds hold against chaos." The poems seem to delineate boundaries or fields of order against chaos, but only seem, because in the larger view Duncan has of poetry and the universe, chaos or disorder are parts of a larger order. The real boundary of this poem, then, is between a state of awareness and its absence. Delineating that boundary, or more fundamentally recognizing the difference, is the responsibility of the poet. In the "disturbance of words within words," the poet's poems are constructs, architectures, flowers which turn into "flames lit to the Lady." The limits and definitions of physical reality must give way before the reality of the visionary imagination. Paradoxes, fairy tales, children's games are not evasions but ways of entry, supralogical confrontations with "what is." Duncan firmly stands in the romantic tradition, which he has identified as "the intellectual adventure of not knowing." In his poetry, then, he will constantly interrogate boundaries, question assumptions, disrupt even the melodies of his own poems in order to participate in the dance, the play of the poem.

In doing so, he demands of his reader a certain tolerance of uncertainty. This opening poem is playful but abrupt, almost orphic. Its title is its first line, and the opening lines must be read, retraced and reread, forcing the reader to reenact the circling and countercircling of the children's game. As he told one interviewer, "I don't have problems with how does it begin, how does it close, because the true form of the thing exists in re-reading it, and re-reading it, and re-reading it" (Balzano 5). The form of this poem, like that of the book, will be *playful, tentative, improvisatory, shadowy.* It is a bound against chaos that invites chaos in as part of the whole—which it is. Duncan delights in tongue-twisting alliteration and ambiguous punctuation, so an unsympathetic reader should be forewarned. But such a reader is also invited. A poem is supposed to be delightful, after all, and the adventure or game attracts us. Duncan demands a great deal of attention to sound, rhythm, and, of course, sense. Attentive readers are rewarded with delight, and with an intellectual adventure.

Developing throughout the book, these images culminate in the final poem of the book, "Food for Fire, Food for Thought," in which Duncan self-consciously comments on the paradox of a last poem in an open poetics: "This is what I wanted for the last poem, / a loosening of conventions and return to open form" (95). The attempt to define or limit is frustrating and necessarily ongoing rather than definitive, but the activity is the poet's preoccupation: "We trace faces in clouds: they drift apart, / palaces of air—the sun dying down / sets them on fire." Fire is the concluding image, again transformed into a flower, as an "unlikely heat / at the edge of our belief bud[s] forth." In these two poems and those in between, Duncan explores the shifting borderlines between essence and form, childhood and adulthood, flame and flower. Like Leonardo, he sees "figures that were stains upon a wall" as he operates "at the edge of belief."

Note first that conventions are loosened, not done away with. To think of "free verse" as completely free of convention would be a mistake, since conventions allow the exchange between poet, poem, and reader to take place. If there were no conventions at all, the poem would be quite literally unreadable, impossible to understand at any level.

The major convention for Duncan is "rime," a concept far more comprehensive than simple end-rhyme, and is informed by his view of the cosmos as a whole. As he told interviewer Howard Mesch:

Rime, or meter, which is the same word in English, is simply a sense of measure being present. And while measure may be like a ruler—12 marks, and all of them equal—a measure actually means you're feeling something did happen before or did not happen before. Any sense of resemblance or any sense of disresemblance indicates the presence of rime. It was taken before, of course, to mean that you have MOON, JUNE. . . . My composition is dependent on how much I feel I am knowing whether something has occurred within an area before. . . . We won't guarantee when it's going to happen. A conventional poem guarantees when it's going to happen, and that's its most important guarantee. When we are no longer centered on convention you have to be aware all the time.

(Mesch 93–94)

Rime is not only a matter of sound, but also of image, emotion, and thought.

Both fire and flower rime, for instance, in the alliterative *f*s and *r*s, but more importantly in their corresponding visual beauty and in their being loci of energy. Both are ephemeral, consuming themselves as they bud or flicker forth. Their identity is reflected in the "green flame" of the opening lines (which again include the title):

> Food for fire, food for thought,
> > good wood
> that all fiery youth burst forth from winter,
> > go to sleep in the poem.
> Who will remember thy green flame,
> > Thy dream's amber?
>
> (95)

Language itself then enters the rime as the theme of permission is again proposed: "Language obeyd flares tongues in obscure matter." The Pentecostal imagery is intentional, as the poet's obedience to the inspiration of the poem brings forth blessings of creative and destructive fire.

The next eleven lines juxtapose images of shadowy figures that the artist and reader must see and join in play. "We trace faces in clouds: they drift apart, / palaces of air" mingles direct and eye rime as the next line echoes the flaming clouds of "Poem Beginning with a Line by Pindar." Runes appear on the sandy sea shore and in stains upon a wall. For the attentive onlooker, permission ("let") to play follows: "Let the apparitions contain in the ground / play as they will." Apprehension, entry into the magical field, awaits anyone sensitive enough to see the significant rimes.

The speaker confuses and then identifies the fragrance of a branch with the sound of its burning on the hearth. More than a simple confusion of the senses (synaesthesia), this is an assertion of identity, of the oneness of the universe, and of its openness to the apprehensive poet. More references to fire and flower than can be summarily explicated follow, to the book's closing lines:

> We are close enough to childhood, so easily purged
> of whatever we thought we were to be,
>
> > flamey threads of firstness go out from your touch.
>
> > Flickers of unlikely heat
> > at the edge of our belief bud forth.
>
> (96)

Returning to the children's ring a round of roses of the book's first poem, these lines return as well to childhood innocence and faith, "easily" purging our adult preconceptions with "flamey threads of first-ness." At the very boundaries of consciousness and rationality, an un-likely belief can bud forth in flame. Even a sensitive paraphrase must be accompanied by an alertness to the ideas of the poem and its atten-tion to rimes of sound and image. This book is major contemporary poetry because its parts so successfully cohere and because it engages us in its vision of oneness and faith.

Individual poems are affected by their context in the whole book, but only a few more can be discussed in any detail. A fine example of Robert Duncan's sense of humor, "Poetry, a Natural Thing" (50) com-pares poetry to salmon and a moose. Without ever trivializing his sub-ject—the nature of the organic poem—Duncan manages to evoke a smile as well as a thought even as he answers what must have been a frustrating rejection he had received from John Crowe Ransom. The poem's opening lines propose, "Neither our vices nor our virtues / fur-ther the poem." Rather than a simple-minded assertion of the amoral-ity of art, Duncan presents as a working proposition his central belief that poetry is a matter of permission, and of submission to forces greater than—and certainly very different from—the poet's own *virtu* or power. Like salmon, "The poem / feeds upon thought, feeling, im-pulse, / to breed   itself, / a spiritual urgency at the dark ladders leap-ing." The interrelatedness of spawning and death will become a recurring theme as Duncan's major poetry realizes more fully than his earlier poetry the nature of organic form.

Even "in the lateness of the world" as we are, we nonetheless respond to those "primordial bellowings / from which the youngest world might spring." This response, however, is "battling, inarticulate," and not a matter of our vices and virtues but of our instinct. "This is one picture apt for the mind," the poem states, and then slips us the sec-ond, "a moose painted by Stubbs" no less. Having shed "last year's extravagant antlers,"

> The forlorn moosey-faced poem wears
>   new antler-buds,
>   the same,
>
> "a little heavy, a little contrived,"

> his only beauty to be
> all moose.

(50)

The quoted line in this passage is drawn from a rejection letter to
Duncan from John Crowe Ransom. In the face of the demands of the
New Critics for irony, ambiguity, and similar intellectual tension,
Duncan can offer only "the forlorn, moosey-faced poem," which just
has to feature a goofy grin. Such *extravagance*—Thoreau's word at that,
extra vagance, going beyond, transgressing—won Duncan few academic
admirers during the heyday of New Criticism. Today this poem, with
its artfully artless mix of self-deprecating moosiness and an earnest
"spiritual urgency," is justly one of his most widely anthologized
poems.

Perhaps the single most important poem in this book is "Poem Beginning with a Line by Pindar," (62–69). Generated by the misreading
of a line from the first Pythian Ode, this four-part poem exemplifies
most of the qualities—thematic and technical—of Robert Duncan's
mature poetry. An apparent jumble at first reading, the Pindar poem
is a collage of allusion, sound, and images that rime internally and that
reverberate throughout *The Opening of the Field*: "*The light foot hears you
and the brightness begins* / god-step at the margins of thought, / quick
adulterous tread at the heart" (62). In the synaesthesia of the first line,
several key motifs appear. The foot-step-tread recurs throughout the
poem, as do the themes of darkness and light and of adultery and love.

Their first occasion is Goya's painting *Cupid and Psyche,* the lovers
whose tale as recounted in Apuleis's *Golden Ass* also informs part 3 of
this poem. Cupid is not the chubby little archer of the Valentine card,
but Eros, physical love, in fact a *daimon* or intermediate being between
the gods and mortals. Love, then, is a power that can bind the human
soul (psyche) to the gods. In the tale, briefly, Psyche's great beauty
caused even the worship of Venus to be neglected. The angry goddess
sent her son, Cupid, to punish Psyche, but he fell in love with her and
made her his wife, though visiting her only at night and forbidding
her to look upon him. Her curiosity overwhelmed her, but when she
saw him in all his glory by lamplight, she was so startled that she
spilled hot oil on his shoulder. He angrily flew away, and she set out
on a journey to find him. She eventually surrendered to Venus in despair and was scourged and given four impossible tasks. With the aid
of several miraculous interventions she accomplished them and was

Francesco Goya, *Cupid and Psyche* (1800–1805). Museum of Barcelona. "In Goya's canvas Cupid and Psyche / have a hurt voluptuous grace / bruised by redemption . . ." ("Poem Beginning with a Line by Pindar").

reunited with Cupid as an immortal. In her quest, Psyche is a figure
of the poet, with Eros as the god-poem.

Duncan's poem calls to our attention the details of the painting,
particularly the copper light falling upon Cupid's body, which provides
illumination or knowledge even as it imposes separation from the loved
one. A brief look at only one stanza serves to highlight Duncan's use
of sound:

> A bronze of yearning, a rose that burns
>   the tips of their bodies, lips,
> ends of fingers, nipples. He is not wingd.
> His thighs are flesh, are clouds
>   lit by the sun in its going down,
> hot luminescence at the loins of the visible.

In the "loosening of conventions" that he advocates, Duncan employs
a subtler use of sound than mere heavy end-rime. In the first three
lines here, "bronze" is echoed by "burns" which also rimes with "yearning," "tips" rimes with "lips" and is heard again in "nipples," and
"fingers" sets up "wingd." Despite the near-rime of "clouds" and
"down," lines four through six are more subtle in their aural pleasures.
The high frontal vowel of "thighs" shifts to the low frontal "clouds,"
"lit" evokes the tips and lips of line two and begins the sequence of
short vowels (including six short *i*s) which, along with the alliterative
*l*s, dominate the final two lines. Psyche's powerful sexual longings for
Cupid, Eros, are rendered in a very physically appealing poetry for
which we have no precise system of notation. Similarly, Cupid's thighs,
seen in the painting as clouds lit by a setting sun, will appear again in
section 4 of this poem and (as we have seen) in the book's final poem.
More such rimes are in this book than can be enumerated, but they
add, quite literally immeasurably, to the delights of reading this book.

In the Pindar poem's second section, the lovers' passion is proposed
as an eternal magic, never to grow old. This thought turns the verse
toward its predecessors, to "the old poets" and "their unaltering
wrongness that has style, / their variable truth." The specific poets he
has in mind include Walt Whitman, William Carlos Williams, Charles
Olson (to whom section 3 is dedicated), and Ezra Pound.

The phrase "their variable truth" alludes to Williams, whose "variable foot" was an innovative poetic convention. The poem mentions "a

stroke"—moving us from Goya's brush stroke to Williams's own stroke, *aphasia,* which had recently crippled him and especially affected his speech. That speech is parodied in the following lines, which open with a pun on the term aphasia itself:

> . . . A phase so minute,
> only a part of the word in-jerrd.
>
> *The Thundermakers descend,*
>
> damerging a nuv. A nerb.
> The present dented of the U
> nighted stayd. States. The heavy clod?
> Cloud. Invades the brain. What
> if lilacs last in *this* dooryard bloomd?
> (63)

"The Thundermakers descend," apparently a continuation of Pindar's ode, fits quite well here. Not only are Williams and the other "thundermakers" physically and inevitably declining, but the verb calls to mind Williams's "The Descent" from *Paterson,* book 2, itself a masterful display of his variable foot and a testimony to the inevitable rightness of the design. Further, Duncan's imitation of Williams's aphasic speech introduces a diatribe against current American policies in an appropriately punning way—the U. S. is presently dented and benighted, clouded with clods, its leadership since 1865 in sharp contrast to Whitman's beloved Lincoln:

> Hoover, Roosevelt, Truman, Eisenhower—
> where among these did the power reside
> that moves the heart? What flower of the nation
> bride-sweet broke to the whole rapture?
> Hoover, Coolidge, Harding, Wilson
> hear the factories of human misery turning out commodities.
> For whom are the holy matins of the heart ringing?
> Noble men in the quiet of morning hear
> Indians singing the continent's violent requiem.
> Harding, Wilson, Taft, Roosevelt,
> idiots fumbling at the bride's door,
> hear the cries of men in meaningless debt and war.
> Where among these did the spirit reside

          that restores the land to productive order?
          McKinley, Cleveland, Harrison, Arthur,
          Garfield, Hayes, Grant, Johnson,
          dwell in the roots of the heart's rancor.
          How sad "amid lanes and through old woods"
             echoes Whitman's love for Lincoln!

                                          (63–64)

The sound rime of the first three lines underlines the disparity between
the flower of the nation and the spiritual power to move the heart and
the dented present of President Eisenhower, himself a recent stroke
victim. Just as the clod/cloud that invades the brain recalls by contrast
the sun-lit cloud-like thighs of Eros, the bride-sweet flower of the
nation with idiots fumbling at her door only emphasizes the distance
from Psyche. The agonizing question, "Where among these did the
spirit reside / that restores the land to productive order?" and the brief
quotation from "Lilacs," section 5, delineate the central contrast between fruitful love and and ravishing sex.

   Even as the poem attests to the continuity of Duncan's poetic tradition—indeed as it enacts that continuity—it laments the disruption
of values that makes poetry and life itself such a struggle for contemporary man. The individual suffers in the context of a society's "meaningless debt and war": "I too / that am a nation sustain the damage /
where smokes of continual ravage / obscure the flame."

   Whitman's "glorious mistake," represented in two lines quoted from
the 1855 preface, is only that his ideal vision of America ("The theme
is creative and has vista") and its poet ("He is the president of regulation") is not actual, is not true in terms of historical realities. This
poet, nonetheless, must strive "to meet a natural measure."

   Section 3, dedicated to Charles Olson, unites the earlier sections'
concerns with earlier poets and the story of Eros and Psyche, linking
them in turn to the idea of the poet as quester or hero. Venus, Cupid's
mother, charged Psyche with four "impossible tasks," completion of
which would prove Psyche worthy of a divine mate. The first was to
sort seeds Venus had scattered—

                    Psyche's tasks—the sorting of seeds
          wheat   barley   oats   poppy   coriander
          anise   beans   lentils   peas   —every grain
                       in its right place
                              before nightfall.

The alignment of the seeds, in the "natural measure" called for in the final phrase of section 2, subtly echoes Whitman's catalogs of facts in *Leaves of Grass* or Emerson's "Hamatreya." The soul must also encounter danger ("must weep / and come near upon death") and must not open Proserpina's box. Thinking to capture the secret of beauty for herself, Psyche is overcome by Melancholy and enters a deadly sleep. In *The Truth and Life of Myth*, Duncan's comments about sleep, will, and poetry illuminate these lines: "dreaming, the Romantics had realized, was involuntary Poetry. The grace of the poem, the voice, comes from a will that strives to waken us from our own personal will or to put that will to sleep." Such a submission, however, is more than a simple surrender. "But that angel of the event of the poem gives the poet both a permission and a challenge. The poet waking from waking takes up the challenge of the voice of the poem and wrestles against sleep, bringing all the watchful craft and learned art into the striving form in order that that much recognition and admission enter into the event. He strives to waken to the will of the poem, even as the poem strives to waken that will" (FC 47–48).

As much as we may be dismayed by Psyche's curiosity, which after all got her into trouble in the first place, we recognize her all too human behavior. The extension of her plight to that of the poet is artful—

> These are the old tasks.
> You've heard them before.
>
> They must be impossible. Psyche
> must despair, be brought to her
> > insect instructor;
> must obey the counsels of the green reed;
> saved from suicide by a tower speaking,
> > must follow to the letter
> > freakish instructions.
>
> (65)

Following such freakish instructions to the letter, the poet can enter the field of the poem. Like Psyche, Ezra Pound at Pisa was helped by ants, and the poem interpolates several brief allusions—most italicized—to the Pisan cantos, especially numbers 74, 76, 82, and 83.

These lines are interrupted by the question "Who? / let the light into the dark? began / the many movements of the passion?" (66). Like

Psyche again, the poet, or any questing hero, illuminates our situation
whether we want it or not, and begins the passion. Whereas "West /
from east men push," the hero "struggles east / widdershins to free the
dawn." One of the few arcane words in this difficult poem, *widdershins*
can be understood in its context, and means moving in a direction
opposite to the usual, especially in a direction contrary to the apparent
course of the sun. Considered unlucky, such motion is irresistible,
nonetheless—the hero "must struggle alone toward the pyres of Day."
The battle of darkness against the light is now on a far more ominous
plane than that of the book's first poem, with its game, with its secret
circle and its "dream of the grass blowing / east against the source of
the sun" (7).

> The light that is Love
> rushes on toward passion. It verges upon dark.
> Roses and blood flood the clouds.
> Solitary first riders advance into legend.
>
> (66)

Eros, desire itself, informs the quest and impels it into the margins of
light and dark. Rimes, both aural and thematic, recall Cupid's thighs
as clouds. Neither moral nor amoral, such a quest is necessary and even
legendary. The mention of legend introduces a few heavily allusive
lines about the West: "Its vistas painters saw / in diffuse light, in
melancholy," quickly drawing together Whitman's vistas, Goya's diffuse light, and Psyche's melancholy. The poem then returns to the
Cupid and Psyche story, but now explicitly identifies Psyche's longing
and travail with the poet's own.

   The fourth section ties directly to the third. Where the third ends
"Cupidinous Death! / that will not take no for an answer," the fourth
begins "Oh yes!" The ominous, adulterous tread at the margin of
thought reappears in the footfall of "the boundary walker." A paren-
thetical explanation does not really explain to the uninitiated that
Duncan and friends lived in a cabin on Maverick Road in Woodstock,
New York, in 1949. As the snow on the roof melted, it sounded as
though a giant were circling the cabin. "That foot," a poetic foot perhaps, "informd / by the weight of all things / that can be elusive" must
be attended to, just as the poem was generated by an attention to a
mistake in reading Pindar. Even at that, what results is "no more than
a nearness to the mind / of a single image."

The poem repeats its affirmation ("Oh yes!") of "this / most dear," a "catalyst force" that brings the sensitive person's attention to bear, and further rimes with the poem's opening lines: "Who is there? O, light the light!" (68). Cupid's apprehension, his avoidance of the light, rimes with Ezra Pound's eager anticipation of the dawn in his prison cage. In the face of the light, opponents fall back. Cupid, or "Lust gives way. The Moon gives way. / Night gives way," and, in a telling pun that illuminates the poem's own progress, "Minutely, the Day gains." Light and love again verge upon the dark.

Unfortunately, the knowledge gained proves to be bitter. Psyche sees her beloved, but in that instant loses him. Similarly, our inexorable advance into self-consciousness causes us to lose that very innocence of which we are now conscious. In lines again calling to mind the opening poem of the book, Duncan powerfully evokes this bitter loss:

> She saw the body of her beloved
>   dismemberd in waking . . . or was it
> in sight? *Finders Keepers* we sang
>   when we were children   or were taught to sing
> before our histories began   and we began
>   who were beloved   our animal life
> toward the Beloved,   sworn to be Keepers.
>
> (68)

A prose passage disrupts the poem completely, and comments on its method. "Pindar's art, the editors tell us, was not a statue but a mosaic, an accumulation of metaphor." The Pindar poem is itself such a mosaic, a collage of pieces of literature, history, fable, and autobiography, which informs and directs the poem. From "everywhere,"

> the information flows
>   that is yearning. A line of Pindar
> moves from the area of my lamp
>   toward morning.
>
> In the dawn that is nowhere
>   I have seen the willful children
>
> clockwise and counter-clockwise turning.
>
> (69)

"Information" is a pun: data, but form-giving data, flows into the poem. The poet's desire merges with Psyche's yearning, as his lamp and hers merge into the dawn, while the willful children play out their widdershins dance.

The third poem in *The Opening of the Field*, "The Law I Love Is Major Mover" (10–11) both states and demonstrates several key aspects of Duncan's poetic principles, the first and most important of which is the paradox that law is essential for freedom as well as for order. Given Duncan's Emersonian faith in the existence of an all-pervasive cosmic design, he is confronted with the age-old questions of freedom and fate, responsibility and necessity: if the universe is ordered and patterned, what freedom is possible for man? If man's freedom is limited, what are his responsibilities?

Paradox, "a moving obscurity" like the Boyg in Ibsen's *Peer Gynt* as the poem states, serves Duncan well in dealing with such issues. The poem opens with a powerful one: "The Law I Love Is Major Mover / from which flow destructions of the Constitution." Law's order disrupts other orders, especially man's—"No nation stands unstirrd." Courtrooms are involved with both judgment and mercy, and men are both masters and servants of the Law.

How can this be? Logically, it cannot. Duncan cites John Adams's words that such mastery/service "requires the continual exercise of virtue / beyond the reach / of human infirmity, even in its best estate." Ever alert to the roots of language, Duncan expects his reader to be alert to Adams's conjunction of human infirmity and virtue, or *virtu*, power. In such a proposition, responsibility too must be redefined as "the ability to respond." Even in his most recent work, Duncan insists on a "poetics of responsibility."

The poet enters the dance now, as the one who must maintain his alertness to the law, to those "freakish instructions" that saved Psyche's life and which, however improbably, brought things into their "natural measure."

The poem proceeds then as a series of responses, its turns and advances and even its hesitations informed by the author's attentiveness to the "sentence"—in both syntactic and judicial senses—of the Law. "The myriad of spiders' eyes that Rexroth saw" leads to the insight that "the universe is filld with eyes then, intensities, / with intent." This in turn leads to the idea of being a witness before the Law, thence to reciprocity, from scales of justice to scales of music, a music that "restores / health to the land." We then return to the original idea of law:

"Hear! Beautiful damnd man that lays down his law lays down / / himself creates hell / a sentence unfolding healthy heaven" (11). Man in his arrogance creates hell in his laws if he violates the "major mover." As such, he "that will not fall upon your face / or upon knees" will be "twisted out of shape, crippled / by angelic Syntax." Destruction brings order, and death brings renewal, just as "the Angel that made a man of Jacob / made Israel in His embrace." The sentence of this Law, both a judgment and a poem, generates those paradoxes of order in disorder and freedom in necessity that evade articulation in logical prose but that render health, order, and love to the "responsible" poet and his readers.

Two poems likely to be quickly read and easily underestimated are "The Ballad of the Enamord Mage" (23–24) and "The Ballad of Mrs. Noah" (24–26). The first poem combines an orphic tone with fairly regular end-rimes and line lengths. According to Duncan, Denise Levertov did not like the poem because "she was aware I was inhabiting the same territory as Edith Sitwell." Another derivation is the *Rubaiyat*. Stanzas proclaiming that "Serpents I have seen bend the Evening Air / Where Flowers that once Men and Women were / Voiceless spread their innocent Lustre" alternate with italicized couplets such as *"I, a poor writer, who knows not / where or wherefor my body was begot."* The idea of the poet as a Mage is perilously close to a precious presumptuousness. "The Ballad of Mrs. Noah" is likewise full of heavy rimes, rhythms, and wordplay (Boa/Noah, Love/Dove), reminiscent this time of children's poems and word games.

The clue is in the playfulness. In the "Enamord Mage," he admits, *"I, late at night, facing the page / writing my fancies in a literal age."* Both poems are fancies, fun to read and not nearly so ponderous as a literal-minded symbol-hunting reader is likely to want to make them. They are games, entertainments of the sort shared by "The Maidens" in the fifties, and should be enjoyed for their delight in language, rhythm, the sensuousness of sound. Beyond that, "Mrs. Noah" enacts a fable or nursery rhyme of "grim humor" (25), in which Crow's "The World is an everlasting Night" is countered by the Dove's "Promise for only Tomorrow": "Ah! the Rainbow's awake / and we will not fail!" Reigning over the drama is Mrs. Noah's tolerant awareness of frail humanity:

Mrs. Noah steppd down
into the same old wicked repenting

Lord-Will-We-Ever recently recoverd
comfortable World-Town.

(26)

While such poems will not please every reader and may very well be
an acquired taste, as such they serve as a warning to the limits of one's
likings or tastes in contemporary poetry, especially in appreciating the
work of a poet so diverse as Duncan. Before dismissing these deceptive
poems as slight, at least come to an understanding of what they are
doing.

Another example of his range, and a more "serious" poem, is "After
Reading *Barely and Widely*" (88–92), a nonmetrical terza rima salute
to Louis Zukofsky. Incorporating numerous quotations and echoes from
Zukofsky's book, the poem investigates the danger of poetry, and its
apprehension is real—not the pretended fear of the preacher who only
pretends to question the foundations of his activity and whom Emerson
scorns in "The Divinity School Address," but rather "the cold sweat of
terror / that's in the double-play of the mind." In such an art, "Uncertainty is root of the gentleness." The poem invests with new force the
cliché of a "dear" or "touching" art:

> *Do not touch.*
> Forbear if you respect the man!
> He who writes a touching line dares over much.
>
> He does not observe
> the intimate boundaries of natural speech
> —then we in hearing must have reserve.
>
> Poetry, that must *touch* the string
> for music's service
> is of violence and obedience a delicate balancing.
>
> (88–89)

This poem serves to emphasize the importance of the context of Duncan's work. Emphasizing his debt to Zukofsky, who remains for Duncan "the master of a salutary art, a call to order" ("Reading Zukofsky"
421), "After Reading *Barely and Widely*" draws out once again Duncan's own central themes: boundaries that must be recognized yet also
crossed, and the poet's service to his art in violence and obedience.

Thus the poem's pivotal rime is of doubling, mirroring, dividing and rejoining, turning away and returning: First in the play on the Greek words ἰδιώτης (a private citizen) and ἰδίω (from ἰδος: to sweat), "the cold sweat of terror / that's in the double-play of the mind too" (88); then to the double meaning of "dear," as used in "a careless hostility and affection" by an old battleaxe, which also faces "two ways / (the rude force, *twegen*)"; then to some "delicate balancings"—of violence and obedience already cited, of Zukofsky and H. D., of the boundary of certitude and "boundless faith," of "good and bad jews, gods / and *baeddel* mixtures" even to Shylock, who "laughs, he bleeds, / he turns both ways, he is a man" (89–90).

At this point Duncan has driven to the heart of his poem, the nature of man as "Shrunken Jehova, cunning Pan! / . . . / Of such double-dealings I would talk" (91). The tension of such contrasts, a "division and union" (92) that generates this poem, anticipates *Bending the Bow*, whose own title metaphor calls for such a paradoxical power. The doublings continue to pile up in unparaphraseable play, into the poem's final six stanzas, which self-consciously close the poem by returning more closely to true end rimes, themselves helping a poem "elsewhere seeming almost to flounder / / helpless into meaning, by rime / restricted." The boundary of form enables the poem, makes it possible—"a discretion circling round / / a containd danger." Such "apprehension" is truly both aware and fearful, a tribute to Zukofsky and a warning.

The Opening of the Field also introduces Duncan's "The Structure of Rime," the first of several continuing long poems. That is, while individual poems of the set are complete, the set itself has not stopped. Duncan has several such poems, the larger implications of which are discussed in the seventh chapter's treatment of "Passages."

A primary fact the reader must keep in mind when considering these sets is that Duncan's work is polysemous. As complex as "The Structure of Rime" and "Passages" are, they are never self-contained units, but rather exist also as parts of the books in which they appear. Thus the first "Structure of Rime" is directly linked to the immediately preceding poem, "The Law I Love Is Major Mover," in its imagery of the poet wrestling with the poem as Jacob wrestled with the angel. The eleventh one relates more directly to the three following poems, also not part of "The Structure of Rime" but forming a separate constellation of their own dealing with such central Duncan themes as boundaries and the ongoing process of destruction and renewal.

As a set of related poems, "The Structure of Rime" does display some identifying characteristics: most, though not all, are in prose; they all deal directly with the nature of poetic language and form; and they contain what Duncan has called "the persons of the language." The first thirteen sections of "The Structure of Rime" appear in *The Opening of the Field* (14 through 21 are in *Roots and Branches;* 22 through 26 in *Bending the Bow*; 27 and 28 in *Ground Work*). "Rime," as we have seen, means far more than similar end sound, and rather is a sense of correspondence. In "The Structure of Rime II," the poet asks, "What of the Structure of Rime?" and is told, "*An absolute scale of resemblance and disresemblance establishes measures that are music in the actual world*" (13). This absolute or all-pervasive scale incorporates discord or opposition as well as similarity ("resemblance and disresemblance") and operates in the actual world rather than as an ideal form.[1] Its pursuit amounts to a "beautiful compulsion" (13), at once longed for and feared.

The first poem of the series tells us, "Writing is first a search in obedience." The poet apostrophizes the sentence—itself ambiguously a construction of words and a judgment against the poet ("a law of words" [12])—asserting, "O Lasting Sentence, / sentence after sentence I make in your image. In the feet that measure the dance of my pages I hear cosmic intoxications of the man I will be" (12), only to be reproved by the voice of the poem for being "a fierce destroyer of images," one who "vomit[s] images into the place of the Law!" (13). The interrogation of the nature of poetic form continues in every poem of the sequence.

The forceful juxtaposition of terror and everyday life that occurs in number 4 delineates another central motif of the sequence. The fear mixed with longing of number 2 emerges again "when you come to the threshold of the stars, to the door beyond which moves celestial terror" (17). Intense alliteration and vowel play draw together images of hearth, earth, heart, and householder, joining "the continual cauldron that feeds forth the earth" to "the heart that comes into being through the blood." At that threshold one apprehends (grasps and fears) "ramifications of the unknown that appear as trials" (17). Similarly, the Master of Rime ascends and descends "into or out of the language of daily life," at once husband, wife, and "breath that leaps forward upon the edge of dying." As in Duncan's earlier poetry, even into domestic scenes poetic apprehension forces itself.

A primary way it does so is through the play of opposites. Just as the Master of Rime is both a husband and a wife, leaping breath at the point of dying, "The Structure of Rime V" juxtaposes black and white, one world and two, life and death, fire and shadow in its "geometry." Since *geo* means "earth" and *meter* means "measure," this poetry literally measures the earth, lays out its field in the dance of tensions thus created. The children playing their games in "Often I Am Permitted" reappear in "The Structure of Rime VI," a poem celebrating joy rather than fear—games, play, and dance.

"The Structure of Rime VII" draws these themes together. Black King Glélé is "a tranquil spirit of pure threat," a figure "of enlarged terror" (20). The poet, however, receives "the counsels of the Wood": *"Lie down, Man, under Love. The streams of the Earth seek passage thru you, tree that you are, toward a foliage that breaks at the boundaries of known things. The measures of Man are outfoldings of Chaos"* (20). In the face of diabolical threat, of annihilating chaos, Man is to serve as the measure and as the pathway (passage) of life. *"In the Dance you turn from your steps cross visibly thru the original mess—messages of created music, imprints, notes, chosen scales, lives, gestures."* In his poetry, albeit "created" and "chosen," sometimes only imprints and notes, "the original mess" is transfigured, clarified, into "messages." As opposed to Glélé, the "tranquil spirit," the poet then declares, "And I stand, stranger to tranquility because I am enamord of song, to sing to Glélé the King as I would sing to relentless history."

Rime itself results, because it "falls in the outbreakings of speech as the Character falls in the act wherefrom life springs, footfalls in Noise which we do not hear but see as Rose pushd up from the stem of our longing" (20). Poetry is as sure as a genetically encoded message. As we again experience poetry synaesthetically—this time we see the footfall's noise, whereas in the Pindar poem the light foot heard—the sexual urge of the poem, most evident in the image of the Rose just cited, is chilled in the final line, Glélé's response: *"I am the Rose."* Fear and desire, apprehension as an act of knowing and as gut level fear, come together in a poetry that is indeed a "stranger to tranquility."

Chapter Six
Roots and Branches (1964)

The title lyric of *Roots and Branches* establishes the book's central metaphor, "the ramifications below and above the trunk of vegetative life," and introduces its primary propositions. "Roots and Branches" is, as well, one of Duncan's most inspired lyrics, a delightful dance in the measure of its subject, the monarch butterfly.

The butterflies' flight, in the speaker's imagination, traces out the shape of a tree—"unseen roots and branches of sense / I share in thought." This is making "sense" with a vengeance, and an effective pun on the word undercuts its materialistic connotations. The butterflies, "messengers of March," are the harbingers of spring, but they are so ephemeral that they present "filaments woven and broken." Nonetheless, their paradoxically "intent and easy" flight—enacted in the alliteration of falling, flowery, floating, flitting, filament, fluttering—evokes the speaker's strong response: "How you perfect my spirit! . . . / awakening transports of an inner view of things." These "unseen roots and branches of sense" promise "casual certainties," and this is no typo for "causal." The fluttering, ephemeral butterflies, in their "intent and easy" profusion, correspond to the speaker's spirit and literally inspire him. The poem's heft is only increased by the qualifying terms "this morning" and "almost" bracketing its climax: "There are / / echoes of what I am in what you perform / this morning. How you perfect my spirit! / almost restore / an imaginary tree of the living in all its doctrines / by fluttering about." The poet's epiphany, inspired by the correspondence between his spirit and the beauty of the common butterfly, denies the "common sense" boundary between physical reality and a transcendent reality. Frank in its romantic idealism, the poem evokes an Emersonian wonder at the harmony of physical and spiritual facts for a modern audience every bit as skeptical as Emerson's neighbors.

The central metaphor of the tree pervades the book: a concern with organic growth and its attendant cycle of budding, coming to fruition, decaying, and going dormant or even dying. Its primary propositions are a poetry that itself participates in a similar organic process; a concern with roots and branches of the poet and his work, or his derivations; and an increasing awareness of the tenacious intrusion of what we might call "an outer view of things," which challenges and even disrupts the poet's "casual certainties" and forces him more directly to address himself to his place in the world. The delightful epiphany provided by the butterflies on that March morning "almost" restored, and then only briefly, that transport of "an inner view of things." As we shall see in the next chapter, the harsh intrusions of the outer view will produce even more sharply political poetry.

As we have already seen, most of Duncan's poetry is very conscious of itself *as poetry,* and as such comments—often directly—on the poetic process. His direct interrogation of the forms and processes of poetry, "The Structure of Rime," continues with eight sections, numbered 14 to 21, in this book. Perhaps most haunting is number 20, in which the Master of Rime tells him, "You must learn to lose heart. I have darkend this way and you yourself have darkend. Are you so blind you cant see what you cant see?" (170). He is told of "the sightless ones" who open windows and listen to the songs outside, and he receives the message "the Mother of this Blindness" has given to them: *"Absence rimes among the feathers of birds that exist only in sight. The songs you hear fall from their flight light like shadows stars cast among you"* (170). Too subtle for our critical language adequately to describe, the second sentence's alliteration and vowel play is simply breathtaking, ample evidence that the poet is attending to these mentors.

The Master of Rime's command, to "let the beat of your heart go. Missing the beat," holds a promise of "bird-notes of a ladder at the edge of the silence" (171). Even the articulation of silence is part of the poet's art, one of the many truths Duncan read in Carlyle's "The Hero as Poet: Dante; Shakespeare" at about this time: "Let us honour the great empire of *Silence,* once more! The boundless treasury which we do *not* jingle in our pockets, or count up and present before men! It is perhaps, of all things, the usefulest for each of us to do, in these loud times."[1]

A poetry of risk is the explicit concern of several other poems. The very title of "Come, Let Me Free Myself" (55), for instance, alerts the reader to a poem dealing with poetics, and indeed the freedom sought is characteristically paradoxical:

> Come, let me free myself from all that I love.
> Let me free what I love from me, let it go free.
> For I would obey without bound,
>   serve only as I serve.

The freedom that leads to obedience becomes a major chord in Duncan's work as he moves into his major achievements, with the theme appearing frequently in "Structure of Rime" and in "Passages." Presenting the image of himself as a hitchhiker, he then asserts, "And how, from one side, / how glad I am no one has come along." Nevertheless, "on the other, I am waiting, / to be on the way, that it be *my* way. / I am impatient." In this internal war, he must fight his own will to dominate: "O let me be free now of *my* way, . . . / For I stand in the way, my destination stands in the way!" The conflict between "the way" and "my way" is that between controlling one's poetry and obeying the Poem or allowing it to lead one.

Such a poetics is fraught with dangers, of course, as the next poem, "Risk" (56–59), acknowledges.

> We cannot divide the costly luster,
> the lovely sheen, from the sound art
>   —quick silver, fool's gold,
>   the mirror flash or the turqoise glaze.
>
> It's not Beauty it must reach, but
>   *towards* Beauty it must reach
>   unsatisfied.
>
> The incorporate dissatisfaction!
>   And that it be rare! beyond our means!
>   to bring life to the risk.

These telling lines recognize the hazards involved, the difficulty of distinguishing good poetry from bad once we discard the conventional criteria of a poetry of control, of regular form. Duncan's essay, "Ideas of the Meaning of Form," published while he was writing this book, directly addressed the problem in the terms of Robert Frost's famous analogy, "I would as soon write free verse as play tennis with the net down." Duncan's response flies in the teeth of such awesome certitude: "But, for those who see life as something other than a tennis game, without bounds, and who seek in their sciences and arts to come into that life, into an imagination of that life, the thought comes that the counterpart of free verse may be free thought and free movement. The explorer displays the meaning of physical excellence in a way different from that displayed by the tennis player" (FC 103). No longer a game, poetry becomes a generative activity of the mind. Rather than trying to ace a serve, the poet rather "scores" the music that he hears, in full recognition that such Beauty is "beyond our means!" "The incorporate dissatisfaction" is a hard burden to bear, but no less than necessary. The satisfactions of conventional form are discounted as the perfections of a game. In their place Duncan chooses perfecting, an ongoing carrying-through that risks everything in a far more serious venture.

Duncan found additional impetus toward this view of the poet as hero, if any were needed, in Carlyle's "The Hero as Poet: Dante; Shakespeare," where he read of Goethe's "open secret" that the world and its laws are there to be read by the hero, as a conqueror, king, philosopher, prophet, or poet (81). Yet more: "while others forget [this divine mystery], he knows it;—I might say, he has been driven to know it; without consent asked of *him,* he finds himself living in it, bound to live in it" (83). Also congenially, Carlyle emphasized the musical qualities of poetry, which he called "*Musical Thought.* The Poet is he who *thinks* in that manner. . . . It is a man's sincerity and depth of vision that makes him a Poet. See deep enough, and you see musically; the heart of Nature *being* everywhere music, if you can only reach it" (84). Duncan shared this confidence in the harmony and design of the universe, what he calls in "Apprehensions" "the given and giving *melos*" (RB 42).

Carlyle's essay discounts the effect or utility of a poet's work on the world ("Effect? Influence? Utility? Let a man *do* his work; the fruit of it is the care of Another than he" [100]) even as it argues that a nation's poets define its greatness longer, even indestructibly, than its laws and riches. At a time when he was struggling with his own role in a troubled nation, Duncan found these words inspiriting.

Perhaps most important, Carlyle provided Duncan with the basic metaphor of *Roots and Branches,* and with support for the generative power of the past. Noting the happy accidents that gave us Dante and Shakespeare, Carlyle adds, "The 'Tree Igdrasil' buds and withers by its own laws,—too deep for our scanning. Yet it does bud and wither, and every bough and leaf of it is there, by fixed eternal laws. . . . It is all a Tree: circulation of sap and influences, mutual communication of every minutest leaf with the lowest talon of a root, with every other greatest and minutest portion of the whole" (102).

Carlyle validated Duncan's strong belief in the informing past, asserting that Dante found his voice in the "ten silent centuries" that preceded him: "The *Divina Commedia* is of Dante's writing; yet in truth *it* belongs to ten Christian centuries, only the finishing of it is Dante's. So always. . . . These sublime ideas of his, terrible and beautiful, are the fruit of the Christian Meditation of all the good men who had gone before him. Precious they; but also is not he precious? Much, had not he spoken, would have been dumb; not dead, yet living voiceless" (98). Likewise Shakespeare's genius came to him unconsciously, natural power manifesting itself "as the oak-tree grows from the Earth's bosom . . . like *roots,* like sap and forces working underground" (108). Duncan continues, in this book, to draw power from the writers of the past, and to define self-consciously his poetic tradition, its roots and branches.

Had he not chosen to reserve the title for a collection of his earlier poems, Duncan might well have called this book *Derivations.* Most of the poems in this book quite explicitly acknowledge their roots in the work of others. Critics who pounce on the negative aspects of this practice fail to recognize Duncan's strong sense of his place in a tradition; consequently they discount his achievement. Some idea of the depth of Duncan's thought can again be found in the notable dichotomies established in his essay "Ideas of the Meaning of Form," published at the time he was writing *Roots and Branches*: "What form is to the conventional mind is just what can be imposed, the rest is thought of as lacking in form. Taste can be imposed, but love and knowledge are conditions that life imposes upon us if we would come into her melodies. It is taste that holds out against feeling, originality that tries to hold out against origins" (FC 104). Taste vs. feeling, and originality vs. origins: in both cases, Duncan comes down firmly on the side of the latter, rejecting what someone once called "originality, the great romantic disease." Our concern, then, should be less with the fact that a poem is derived from another than with the sort of poem that results.

Duncan's adaptation of Shelley's "Arethusa" (78–81) proves instructive, first because Shelley's poem itself re-presents an ancient Greek fable recounted also in Ovid's *Metamorphoses.* In *Caesar's Gate,* Duncan speaks of the "world of Ovid's *Metamorphoses,* of elusive calls and disturbing premonitions of chthonic powers" (xxviii).[2] Arethusa was a nymph pursued even under the ocean by Alpheus, the river-god, until

Artemis changed her into a fountain on Ortygia, an island near Sicily. Shelley wrote the song for a short drama by his wife, Mary. Both Shelley and Duncan are faithful to the original, but their differences are more significant than their similarities.

Shelley's poem has five stanzas of eighteen lines, each made up of six tercets with two lines of anapestic dimeter and a third of anapestic trimeter. To this lightly trotting rhythm Shelley married a regular rime pattern: a a b c c b d d e f f e, etc. Popular conventions of that time, such poetry is far from organic form. Indeed, Shelley used the same meter and rime pattern in "The Cloud."

Duncan completely recasts the poem. Both meter and regular rime are abandoned, and the stanzas are of uneven length. Duncan's first stanza, like Shelley's, depicts the original Arethusa at play in the Acroceraunian mountains. The first change is startling. Duncan tells the tale in the present tense, heightening the action. Avoiding Shelley's regular and predictable rimes (mountains / fountains, streams / gleams), Duncan's measures reflect the sense of the lines. Enabling him to avoid such lines as Shelley's "She leapt down the rocks, / With her rainbow locks / Streaming among the streams," this freedom from regular meters allows a pace that corresponds with the sense, as in the final lines of the first stanza: "As if still asleep she goes, glides or / lingers in deep pools." The alliteration of *l*s and *s*s and the long vowels help with this effect as well.

The firm opening of the second stanza announces the forceful entry of Alpheus. The repetitions of sound (*au* and *o,* particularly) underline his relentlessness, even as the lines' appearance on the page depicts his descent:

> Now bold Alpheus
> aroused from his cold glacier
> strikes the mountains and opens
> a chasm in the rock . . .
>   (78)

Duncan's third and subsequent stanzas draw out the sexual implications of the pursuit in more explicit terms than Shelley's. "White Arethusa, / the sunlight still virginal in her courses," flees from Alpheus and enters "the Dorian / brackish waters," pursued by Alpheus, "close upon her, in gloom, / staining the salt dark tides." Where Shelley has him "rush behind" her, in Duncan's poem he "comes." Where

Shelley presents an unfortunate rime in "Alpheus rushed behind,— /
As an eagle pursuing / A dove to its ruin," Duncan retains the analogy
but provides a rime that aptly links its subjects: "Alpheus / eagle-eyed
down streams of the wind pursues / dove-winged Arethusa."

Duncan's fourth stanza opens with a subtle chiasmus of vowels (another appears in the fifth stanza) that is simply unavailable to Shelley's
brief lines: "Under those bowers they go / where the ocean powers /
brood on their thrones" (79–80). Duncan retains Shelley's image of
weaving "a network of colord lights" as the two, transformed now into
fountain and river, intermingle, and his subsequent line lets us hear
Alpheus's relentless pursuit in the repetition of three of the four final
syllables: "girl-stream and man-river after her." Duncan then extends
the white-black imagery—"Pearl amid shadows / of the deep caves"—
and the sexual imagery also: "—he overtaking her, / as if wedding,
surrounding her, / spray rifts in clefts of the shore cliffs rising. / /
Alpheus, / Arethusa, / come home." At this point the differences are
marked. Instead of the union's being perceived as a violation, it is a
coming home. Not only does "coming" retain its sexual meaning, but
the final line reads as a prayer as much as a description.

Thus, Duncan's final stanza is again more clearly sexual, as "Arethusa to Alpheus gladly comes." Their union is echoed in another
chiasmus:

> Into one morning two hearts awake,
> at sunrise leap from sleep's caves to return
> to the vale where they meet,
> drawn by yearning from night into day.
> (80)

Arethusa's apprehension—fearful and also coming to know, even in
the sexual sense—itself is depicted in the imagery of this book's two
most important poems, "Apprehensions" and "The Continent," about
which more later. Her union, in Duncan's poem, is no ravishing:
"Down into the noontide flow, / into the full of life winding
again. . . ," the lovers' winding journey is apparently one reference for
the title of the second part of this book, "Windings." Yet more: where
Shelley left them in an inhuman suspension ("like spirits that lie / In
the azure sky / when they love but live no more"), Duncan's final stanza
closes with imagery of a natural cycle of separation and ecstatic re-
union, "seeking their way to love once more."

Duncan's use of Shelley is most appropriate. Not only are both clearly "romantic" poets, part of a tradition of idealism. Duncan's openness to other writers provides him entry into a larger field of poetry, what Shelley himself called "that great poem, which all poets, like the co-operating thoughts of one great mind, have built up since the beginning of the world." Duncan's poem, "set to new measures," renews the myth for his modern audience and provides graphic evidence that in such evolutions poetry is, indeed, "a natural thing."

Another derived poem, "Cyparissus," Duncan identifies as being drawn from Ovid's *Metamorphoses,* and he even identifies the translator and the date (Henry T. Riley for Bohn's Library in 1902). The metamorphosis of Cyparissus into a tree is an apt subject for *Roots and Branches,* but Duncan characteristically investigates the fable as an "evidence of the real," raising larger questions about what poetry is and what it is to be human. "How did you wound him?" Duncan asks, following Riley's translation into the direct address. "It is / as if man had great need of some agony, / for the youth Cyparissus, / knowing, yet unknowing, / pierced the lordly heart with his spear." Because the youth so loved the stag, the wound is self-destructive, and the repercussions still affect both poets and the reader:

> so that now as the god Orpheus sings
> his song remembers the grief of that wound.
> I too, drawing the story again from Ovid's pen,
> know the bewildering knowledge in the beast's gaze
> that searcht with trust his lover's eyes
> and found his own wound repeated there.

(165–66)

Anticipating the central metaphor of *Bending the Bow,* the union of the poet's lyre and the soldier's bow, Duncan writes,

> Apollo's art
> that from the lyre
> sends notes to pierce the human soul
> from which the life of music flows
> sends the arrow from the bow.

It seems to the poet that "the deep of the god's light / is a cup that needs man's weeping to be filld." Like Orpheus, "deriving his art from

what men suffer," the poet must "strike at the heart / to make his
song." This poem that branches out from the ancient fable has deep
roots, revealing again not only Duncan's *use* of the resources of generations of his masters, but also his deeply human sense of the role of the
poet.

Duncan is equally responsive to his contemporaries. First published
by Denise Levertov in *O Taste and See* (1964), "Claritas" was apparently
enclosed in a letter she sent to Duncan. In the poem, "The All-Day
Bird, the artist," strives "in hope and / good faith to make his notes /
ever more precise, closer / to what he knows."[3] The bird prays, then,
for a full, round first note, and for subsequent notes to be as fine as
sweetgrass, as the tail of a lizard, as a leaf of chives. The poem closes
with two remarkable stanzas, the last one presenting the bird's song:

V

The dew is on the vineleaves.
My tree
is lit with the
break of day.

VI

Sun
light.
        Light
light light light.

Duncan's response, "Answering (after 'Claritas' by Denise Levertov)"
(124–26), is both admiring and chiding. His poem begins, "A burst /
of confidence. Confiding / / a treasured thing . . ." (124). With more
faith than hope (*confidere,* etymologically), Duncan's poet sings a different song. Incorporating the workmen's tools as well as the bird's
song, which they "punctuate," this poem exclaims, "They are employd
/ at making up a joyous / / possibility. / / They are making a living /
where I take my life." In response to Levertov's striving for precision,
for a closeness "to what he knows," Duncan proposes instead a "responsibility," quite literally an ability to respond to "the rise of words."
Instead of the artist's prayer, Duncan insists on an obedience to what
here he calls "the natural will":

> For joy
> breaks thru
>
> insensible to our human want.
> Were we birds too
>
> upon some blowing crown of seeds,
> it would be so
>
> —we'd sing as we do.
>
>   (126)

The poem is derived, as an answer to another poem, but in no way is it less powerful for that. Duncan and Levertov have had a long and fruitful, if sometimes stormy, friendship. His response to her poem indicates his concern with origins of song, rather than a personal originality. Trusting one's intuitive sense to discover "the real" involves very real dangers, greater than simply failing or looking foolish. This is a raging war of the imagination "between its energy that is a disorder seeking higher intensities and its fate or dream of perfection that is an order where all light, heat, being, movement, meaning and form, are consumed toward the cold" (FC 89). Absolute, energetic disorder and absolute, frozen entropic stasis—apprehension or awareness of the reality of these propositions generates an awe-full apprehension or fear in the exploring poet and reader.

Such concerns are directly addressed in the aptly named "Apprehensions" and in "The Continent," two poems even more closely related to each other than are all of Duncan's poems. The central theme of "Apprehensions" is that which "defines the borderlines of the meaning." Its opening chord, "To open Night's eye that sleeps in what we know by Day" (30), announces the familiar concerns with overcoming common sense and sensory limitations, and with the assertion of a paradoxical oneness. Quotidian preoccupations obstruct our perspective and limit our perceptions. In sharp contrast, the "Sage Architect" awakens "the proportions and scales of the soul's wonder" (34) and lets light and shadow mix. The poem is a song to apprehension—both fearful and perceiving—of excavation of boundaries, resemblances, rimes. The central apprehension is of concordances that overcome our limited sense of shifting time, place, and boundaries in favor of an overriding order.

Virtually any passage selected at random would illuminate this general overview with particulars. In the first section, excerpts from "Renaissance Cosmologies" by Paul-Henri Michel intertwine with Duncan's dream images and his reactions to both. Speaking to the reader as well as to Duncan, the poem demands, "You've to dig and come to see what I mean" (31). Michel tells Duncan of Ficino's theory that "life circulates from the earth / to the stars / *'in order to constitute the uninterrupted / tissue of the whole of nature'"* (31). Duncan's mind "falls away" from the text, deriving "only a gleam" and refusing to "bring the matter to light" (31). According to George Quasha, "Apprehensions" was "a reluctant composition, because of his wish to avoid or forget the dream behind it. . . . Personal resistance becomes textual disjunction and reordering."[4]

The disturbing imagery of the earth as something animate, of excavations resembling graves, of the earth as "a great toad-mother, / a fancy figure of Tiamat, / pitted with young" and of glances of what "might have been a living thing" in the muck, "the shit-yellow clay"—such imagery brings apprehension, again in both senses:

> And the soul was reveald where it was,
> fearful, rapt, prepared to withdraw
>   from knowing,
> looking down from the six-foot pit where . . .
>   (32; Duncan's ellipses)

The second section offers a "directive," that "the architecture of the sentence / allows / personal details, portals / reverent and enchanting, / constructions from what lies at hand / to stand / for what rings true" (32–33). Rather than being obscure, the poet's intensely personal images and anguish are portals, windows and entrances into *What Is,* into the field. Constructions, whether built by architects or by poets, establish fictive limits and spaces by which we come to apprehension and which must be apprehensively superseded. The themes of permission, of the architecture of the sentence, and of the composing process as an ongoing interaction between the poet and the poem all call to mind the ongoing series "The Structure of Rime," and indeed the fourth section of "Apprehensions" is "The Structure of Rime XIV."

All the aspects of the poem, from the "dream or vision" of our grandfathers' fathers to the child's play of love and death that rimes with the poet's play as well as with World War I, move in section 3 as "part by part / the cast, a bit in the play, / of the eyes, of the dice, of design toward crisis" (37). Duncan's faith in a cosmic design is firm, but that design is not necessarily what a man or a poet might want it to be. Where Frost chose to encounter this demon in traditional forms, Duncan tellingly opens his poem up into a sequence of intricately related meditations, in the fifth and final segment culminating in "the living apprehension, the given and giving *melos*" (42). After these haunting dreams of caves, worms, and graves, Duncan reports in his poem that, on 27 March, "we found after the rains a cave-in along the path near the rosemary and thyme, disclosing the pit of an abandond cess pool. Because of the dream fragment a month before, the event seems to have been anticipated. A verification of the caves seen in actual life after they had appeard in the life of the poem" (42). This report is immediately followed by the line "Wherever we watch, concordances appear," then a litany of "orders," none of them final, and the strong closure: "There is no life that does not rise / melodic from scales of the marvelous. / / To which our grief refers" (43). Faith and grief, like order and disorder, are interwoven, and this poetry tries to apprehend "the borderlines of the meaning." As explorers rather than as tennis players, Duncan and his readers meet among the powers of "a god of the time where the cards fall." Such a poetry acknowledges that "All things are powers within all things," but men are reduced to "their few words." Readers must attend not to "what they think they are saying," but to "the thing they are telling" (41). Such a journey is fearful yet exhilarating, an apprehension of the given and giving melos.

Roots and Branches closes with the closely related sequence "The Continent," in which Duncan directly accepts and names his role as "the artist of the margin" who "works abundancies" and who recognizes that the scope of poetry "needs vast terms" because it is "out of earthly proportion to the page" (172). On the literal level, Duncan calls for a long poem that, like Whitman's, will be creative and have vista. Metaphorically and more significantly, he is calling for a poetry on the edge of consciousness, an expanding awareness of "marginal" realities, an openness to unusual or unconventional apprehensions. Unlike the coastal resident's awareness of the alien or the other, "The mid-Western mind / differs in essentials." Without Buddhist temples or variant ways of seeing, midwesterners "stand with feet upon the ground / against the / run to the mythic sea, the fabulous" (173). This is not praise for Antaeus.

The poem continues, describing a sparrow smashed upon a sidewalk.

More than an allusion to William Carlos Williams's famous poem, the passage illuminates the difference between having a perspective in space and time and being "too close / for shadow, / the immediate!" (174). The central image of the poem, the continent (or variously, Gaia or earth), itself examines horizons, especially those between shore and land and night and day. Two explicit connections between "Apprehensions" and "The Continent" are the idea that "we conquer life itself to live" (36, 173), and that the earth's rotation at once embodies boundaries, transgresses them, and so extends a promise of life and resurrection. Compare this passage from "Apprehensions" with the following one from "The Continent":

> It is the earth turning
> that lifts our shores from the dark
> into the cold light of morning,
> eastward turning,
> and that returns us from the sun's burning
> into passages of twilight and doubt,
> dim reveries and gawdy effects.
> The sun is the everlasting center of what we know,
> a steady radiance.
>
> The changes of light in which we dwell,
> colors among colors that come and go,
> are in the earth's turning.
>
>   (39–40)

*   *   *

> It's still Saturday
> before Easter
> and Love's hero lies
> in the nest of our time.
> . . . .
> Effeminized, the soul is Sleeping Beauty
> or Snow White who waits
> for Sunday's kiss to wake her.
> Time zone by time zone
>
> across the continent dawn so comes
> breaking the shell of flowers

> a wave
> Earth makes in turning
> a crest
> against tomorrow breaks.
>
>   (175–76)

Linking the imagery of continent and ocean, night and day with Easter
(evidently the actual time of the writing of the poem), the poem denies
any clear distinction, even between life and death.

As Duncan's "The Law" proposes, "There are no / final orders. But
the Law / constantly destroys the law" (26). Far from fragmenting our
beliefs and dissociating our sensibilities, such a vision asserts the oneness of things: one time, one god, one promise flaring forth from "the
margins of the page." In the apparent chaos of flux and change—"moving in rifts, churning, enjambing"—both continent and poem testify
to a dynamic unity. The roots and branches interconnect throughout.
Again, at the border, at the edge of meaning, like Columbus we find
not the abyss but new worlds.

Chapter Seven
Bending the Bow (1968)

Duncan followed *Roots and Branches* four years later with yet another major book, *Bending the Bow*. A response to a violently turbulent era, the book projects a deeply concerned "political" poetry and, at the same time, it manifests in "The Passages Poems" Duncan's fullest realization to date of the possibilities of poetry. His introduction to the book directly addresses the issue the of poet's role in the world that had been anticipated in *Roots and Branches*. The term "political poetry" must be understood in a particular sense here. Avoiding propagandistic diatribes, Duncan's poetry is informed, once again, by etymology: "political poetry" is, for him, poetry concerned with the *polis,* the city, and what it means to be a good citizen.

When Duncan's introduction, which discusses his poetry with his accustomed insight, criticizes the war in Vietnam he deals with it in both global and personal terms. The war itself is foolish, based on false boundaries: "a war, then, as if to hold all China or the ancient sea at bay, breaks out at a boundary we name *ours.* It is a boundary beyond our understanding" (i). Captured by a rigid form, by a fixed image of ourselves, we are unable to adapt to new conditions and insights. In contrast, the pulse of the poet "beats before and beyond all proper bounds." Not content with such a disengaged overview, however, Duncan presents us with the second part of his introduction, "The Readers." Clearly based on an autobiographical experience, it recounts the violent confrontation between a group of protesters, including Duncan, and some young soldiers, presumably National Guardsmen. Their "refusal to give even the beginnings of a hearing" is itself "the nature of all dying orders, a death so strong we are deadend to the life-lines." But as moving as the confrontation is, its title links the soldiers with "the hostile readers" who, similarly deadened, also refuse to give a hearing. The reader unprepared for and unsympathetic to this kind of poetry is warned: "Out of order, we can no longer move them to consider that our liberties are obediences of another order that moved us. We ourselves are the boundaries they have made against their humanity." In the face of such seriousness, and of such an intense involvement in the life around him, it is incredible that some critics have high-handedly dismissed Duncan's work as precious, abstract, and (a derogatory remark, this) "too intellectual." This book alone effectively refutes such charges.

The book's title establishes the contrasts of bow and lyre, war and music, Apollo and Hermes, whose tension generates this book's field. Duncan speaks of the poem not as a stream of consciousness but as an area of composition in which "the poet works with a sense of parts fitting in relation to a design that is larger than the poem" and which he knows "will never be completed" (vi). While such a view of poetry goes contrary to traditional expectations of the tightly formed, carefully closed poem, it opens possibilities for an emotionally and intellectually adventurous poetry.

The title lyric develops the bow and lyre analogy which articulates the central Heraclitean themes of design, connection, and unity in diversity: "At the extremity of this / design / 'there is a connexion working in both directions, as in / the bow and the lyre'" (7). The quoted phrase is directly from Heraclitus' *The Cosmic Fragments* number 51 (203–21) and Duncan elaborates in his introduction: "Hermes, god of poets and thieves, lock-picker then, invented the bow and the lyre to confound Apollo, god of poetry. . . . The part in its fitting does not lock but unlocks; what was closed is opend" (iv). The maturation of these primary themes of Duncan's poetry constitutes *Bending the Bow,* and particularly the "Passages Poems," as his greatest book, for it is in their development that Duncan's definition of poetry itself, here cited from his essay of the same period, "Towards an Open Universe" (1966), is fully realized: "It is not that poetry imitates but that poetry enacts in its order the order of first things, as just here in this consciousness, they may exist, and the poet desires to penetrate the seeming of style and subject matter to that most real where there is no form that is not content, no content that is not form" (FC 81). Rather than imitating an external, objective reality (whatever that might be), the poem enacts what Duncan calls "this most real," and is in fact "our primary experience of it" (FC 78). The turn and return (verse, from *versus,* "turning") of poetry are phases of a dynamic unity, just as are the alterations of day and night or the systole and diastole of the heart. The focus of his poetry and poetics remains on the intensity of the point of transition.

"Bending the Bow" articulates at the outset that faith and that apprehension:

> We've our business to attend Day's duties,
> bend back the bow in dreams as we may
> til the end rimes in the taut string
> with the sending.
>
> (BB 7)

This evocative poem moves from an absentminded daydream into an intuitive awareness of some mysterious presence that can only be hinted at with ellipses or named "ghostly exhilarations" (BB 7). Whereas "the hostile readers" confronted in Duncan's introduction to this book would suppress such intuitions, Duncan refuses to exclude anything, asserting that "the artist of abundancies" finds nothing "out of order" since "all orders have their justification finally in an order of orders only our faith as we work addresses." Even though the presence at the borders of the poem is troubling, Duncan accepts and even praises it: "Praise then the interruption of our composure, the image that comes to fit we cannot account for, the juncture in the music that appears discordant" (BB ix–x).

Even the "litter / of coffee cups and saucers" on a table enters such a poem, because Duncan is a poet of the immediate present as well as of cosmic realities. A number of Duncan's detractors accuse him of an intellectual distance that leaves his poetry abstract and emotionless, but this is a false distinction and a fatuous argument. In reality, his poetry is charged with emotion and immediacy, as he is fully aware. To cite "Towards an Open Universe" one final time: "The imagination of this cosmos is as immediate to me as the imagination of my household or my self, for I have taken my being in what I know of the sun and of the magnitude of the cosmos, as I have taken my being in what I know of domestic things" (FC 76). In practice, the poet must be attentive to the presence of "this most real" in the quotidian details of his life, for they provide him with passages to a transcendent awareness: "This presentation, our immediate consciousness, the threshold that is called both *here-and-now* and *eternity*, is an exposure in which, perilously, identity is shared in resonance between the person and the cosmos" (83).

"The Passages Poems"

While the propositions of this ambitious poetry had been manifest in Duncan's work for years, they fully flowered in his grand achievement, "The Passages Poems." Twentieth-century poets have been drawn to the long poem as if by compulsion: Pound's *Cantos*, Williams's *Paterson*, Eliot's *The Waste Land* and *Four Quartets*, Olson's *Maximus Poems*, Crane's *The Bridge*, Roethke's "North American Sequence," Stevens's "Notes toward a Supreme Fiction," Ginsberg's *Howl* and "These States," to name only a handful. As different as these poems are, each attests to the obsession our poets have with the major poem, the substantial achievement on a large canvas, with all its attractions and attendant difficulties. "Passages," Robert Duncan's major work to date, is a long poem generative of ideas yet alive to immediate experience. Combining lyricism with scope and intensity with amplitude, "Passages" consists so far of over forty poems, at once independent entities and interdependent through their relation to a central proposition and to the rest of Duncan's work.

When published in book form, a long poem is presented by the poet as an encompassing vision. Even if a hallmark of such a poem is that it is unfinished—as with the *Cantos* or *Paterson*—its publication in sections with imaginative coherence argues for a certain wholeness or comprehensiveness of vision. Duncan has explicitly refused to collect "Passages" into one book, however, and their appearance amid other poems constitutes an important element in the reader's experience. "Passages" opens with an essential experience, dovetails into a second poem, and so on. Duncan "works with all parts of the poem as *polysemous*, taking each thing of the composition as generative of meaning, a response to and a contribution to the building form" (BB ix). With each return to the set, new directions emerge and new facets of earlier poems appear. The process continues with almost unlimited possibilities, terminating only in the poet's death, again like the *Cantos* or *Paterson*.

Despite such powerful derivations as Pound, Eliot, Williams and Olson, "Passages" carves its own place as a decidedly different kind of long poem. His metaphors for the poem—field, collage, mobile, constellation—emphasize parts in relationship, an insistence on the interrelatedness of all things in one grand design. The appearance of the first thirty "Passages" in *Bending the Bow* emphasizes not their sepa-

rateness but their integral relationship to the other poems of that book.
The first stanza of "Structure of Rime XXIII," appearing as it does
between the seventh and eighth "Passages," offers a gloss on the entire
set:

> Only passages of a poetry, no more. No matter how many times the cards
> are handled and laid out to lay out their plan of the future—a fortune—only
> passages of what is happening. Passages of moonlight upon a floor.
>
> (BB 23)

To think of these passages as incidents, fragmentary occurrences, experiences in the life of the poet and the reader, is to grasp the extent
of their modernity. On the most obvious level, we are dealing with
passages "of a poem larger than the book in which they appear" and
belonging "to a series that extends in an area larger than my work in
them" (BB v).

The title suggests entry, a passage into the field of the poem, into
an apprehension (again in the dual sense of awareness and fear) of a
larger reality, into vision. Still, "Passages" should not be confused with
spatial form, despite the references to the field of the poem, because,
as Joseph Frank suggests, spatial form produces resolution and "Passages" is by definition "without bounds."[1] Where Frank emphasizes
spatial recurrence and repetitions that bind a work together, Duncan
gives us recurrences and antagonisms that serve to break up the poem
and destroy its boundaries. Duncan's cosmology forbids that perfection
of form demanded by conventional ideas of art and meaning. He accepts that the field of meanings cannot be realized in poetry, because
"the actual realized poem is just the one form that it is" (FC 50). The
great field can only be suggested by a small field, set up among various
poems or parts of poems. While reality is process, no single poet occupies the total area.

Some differences are apparent between "Passages" and, say, Duncan's
most nearly comparable set, "The Structure of Rime." The latter is
dominated by high prose and includes a number of Rimbaud imitations. Individual poems often present "persons of the poem" who speak
as masks (the Master of Rime, the Messenger in the guise of a Lion,
the Old Woman) in the process of investigating the skeleton of the
poem. Ian W. Reid has called "The Structure of Rime" "prose-poem
propositions . . . to which 'Passages' provide the verse counterpart."[2]
"Passages," on the other hand, is a more fully scored verbal poem, a

series of performance pieces. Indeed, while reading, Duncan will stroke his hand in the air as if conducting them. The voice of the poem speaks directly, without the masks of "The Structure of Rime" (or of Pound's Odysseus, or Olson's Maximus). "Passages" is also Duncan's densest work, particularly in its use of other materials (he delights in calling attention to his thievery, Hermes-like) and of personal memories and allusions. He even provides a bibliography at the end of *Bending the Bow,* but has playfully admitted, "I am also a little *méchant* and quote from an imaginary book."[3]

Despite such distinguishing qualities of "Passages," Duncan's entire canon is interwoven, part and parcel of a coinherent (a word he learned from novelist Charles Williams) vision of poetry and reality. Some "Passages" belong to other sets: "An Illustration: Passages 20" is also "Structure of Rime XXVI"; "Passages 36" is the eighth poem in "A Seventeenth Century Suite." The three poems that precede "The Fire: Passages 13" set up that poem by directly anticipating its general themes and specific imagery. "The Currents: Passages 16" is almost unintelligible out of context, its first line a response to the previous two poems, Verlaine imitations. "Transgressing the Real: Passages 27" picks up the theme of the mating of opposites ("separating and joining, ascending a ladder of litanies") of the preceding poem, "An Interlude."

Such references could be multiplied. Note that "Passages" is not interrupted by other poems, but is continuous as thought or dream. In Whitehead's terms, "The continuum is present in each actual entity, and each actual entity pervades the continuum."[4] To circumvent our preconceived notions of the seriality of becoming, Duncan has stopped numbering "Passages" in favor of Whitehead's "presentational immediacy," which "gives no information as to the past or the future. It merely presents an illustrated portion of the presented duration. It thereby defines a cross-section of the universe" (PR 195). Such an insistence on the present moment for what it is describes a passage.

In Whitehead's cosmology, "Nature is never complete" (PR 340), and, as discussed in chapter 3 above, with such a worldview Duncan has developed an evolutionary poetics. Whitehead also contends that all nature is interrelated, that every facet of reality affects every other facet it comes into contact with. This notion of the complicated interrelatedness of all experience generates for Duncan the concept of the poem as a field of activity that is entered by the poet. The entrance is momentary, a matter of "permission." It is quite literally a passage through experience, a paradoxical attempt to fix ceaseless change. Each

entry adds another perspective on the whole that is happening. For
Duncan, the possibilities have become literally infinite, a prospect at
once exhilarating and threatening.

Whitehead's ideas of process and order illuminate the nature of "Passages" as "cross-sections of the universe," discrete entities in a complex
interrelated whole, in an "endlessly elaborating poem" as Wallace Stevens says in "An Ordinary Evening in New Haven." The set's epigraph
from Julian the Apostate sets forth the proposition of a boundless
poem: "*And Attis encircles the heavens like a tiara, and thence sets out as
though to descend to earth. / • / For the even is bounded, but the uneven is
without bounds and there is no way through or out of it*" (BB 9). Duncan is
attracted by Julian's humanity and empathy, as opposed to what Julian
saw as the inhumanity and monstrous megalomania of Christianity. At
the same time, Duncan's interest is with the uneven, the boundless,
and the irregular, though it is informed by a supreme confidence in
the ultimate orderliness of the universe, which transcends human
awareness. In contrast to Julian's dread of the variable, the plural, and
the unlimited, Duncan will celebrate those very qualities.

"Tribal Memories: Passages 1" introduces "Her-Without-Bounds,"
a feminine principle liable to such various interpretations as the imagination, the Muse, or the Mother. The setting is a City, significantly
capitalized, a central proposition of an ideal society; Duncan has said,
"a poem is a society in words" (NPF). This ideal community recurs in
many "Passages," often under siege as in "The Fire" and in "Moving
the Moving Image: Passages 17," where it appears as Egypt, an ideal
that is passing from man's memory. Here the City is the locus of "the
Eternal" and "the company of the living" (BB 9). The poet is not an
oracle presenting the voice of god; rather, he is part of our local human
community, our household. When reading, Duncan stresses the *h*s to
emphasize the words. The poem's domestic imagery is another major
motif of the set, and Duncan for all his knowledge of mystic lore remains a very domestic poet. In "Orders: Passages 24," the entire creative system is identified as "the great household" and in "The Feast:
Passages 34" even a recipe occurs. The encyclopedic range of "Passages"
is designed to include all of life. Too many readers are misled by Duncan's eclecticism, abstraction, and allusiveness, reading him as a poet
of otherness rather than of the here and now.

The female figure is next extended as Mnemosyne, Memory, the
"Mother with the whispering / featherd wings." The poet speaks of
returning to "her egg, / the dream in which all things are living, /

. . . leaving my self." Two key themes arise immediately, dream and boundary. Leaving the self for the dream is a proposition contra Whitman, until one realizes that the isolated individual is never fully whole until he enters into the communal identity. "I used to *make up* dreams," he tells us in "An Illustration: Passages 20," but now he has surrendered such control and entered a larger form. The egg conjures key images:

> I am beside myself with this
> > thought of the One in the World-Egg,
> enclosed,   in a shell of murmurings,
>
> > > rimed round,
> > > sound-chamberd child.
> > > > > > (BB 10)

Even such brief quotations highlight the play of sound characteristic of the set. Such return-to-the-womb revery sounds the first chord of the major theme of limitation, boundaries, and immediately calls forth its opposite, the crossing of such boundaries:

> It's that first!   The forth-going to be
> > bursts into green as the spring
> > winds blow watery from the south
> and the sun returns north.
> > > > > (BB 10)

This first poem ends in a hypnagogic revery, characteristic of the poet's typical manner of proceeding (compare "A Poem Beginning with a Line by Pindar" and "In the Dark: Passages 36," as well as FC 34), but suitable as well for closing the poem since it blurs another boundary, that between sleep and waking.

Duncan told one audience that "Where It Appears: Passages 4" "really . . . told me what was in the poem" (NPF). At this point he began numbering "Passages," which had only been named until then. His opening lines tease both writer and reader with their "momentous inconclusions." Indeed, the poem's inconclusiveness is momentous, a matter of the boundless energies of the poem becoming endlessly generative of ideas. Such inconclusiveness is not meaningless but momentous, of the moment. "Passages 4" typifies Duncan's delight in poetry

as an energy construct, a dance in process, both visually as it appears
on the page and in the play of vowels, consonants, and freshly perceived correspondences or rimes.

Further, Duncan realizes that he is "statistically insignificant" (BB
15) precisely because, as in "Tribal Memories," he is not an oracle but
a man. Each man, like a star or sun, has an order of his own, an
interrelatedness with all things. In "In the Place of a Passage 22" he
says,

>   Grand Mother of Images,   matrix
>   genetrix,   quickening in rays
>   from the first days of the cosmos,
>
>   turning my poet's mind in tides of
>   solitude, seductive reveries, fears, resolves, outrage
>   yet
>   having this certain specific agent I am
>   (BB 75)

This selflessness is self-creative, humanistic in spite of the apparent
submergence of the self in the larger order. This central paradox of
Duncan's poetics carries some familiar echoes, whether one thinks of
the New Testament or the later Emerson, who built altars to Beautiful
Necessity. The poet is he who integrates the manifold impressions of
an apparently disorderly experience. In doing so, he is a "certain specific agent" of this Grand Mother of Images, literally Her-Without-
Bounds brought however briefly and partially within the compass of a
poem.

Probability, then, is suspended in the closing lines "as if" the poet
could surround the boundless with a shadow. Thus the poet's recognition at the end of the poem:

>   as if I could cast a shadow   •
>
>   to surround,   •
>
>   what is boundless   •
>
>   as if I could handle • this pearl • that touches
>
>   upon every imagination of what

I am •

   wrong about the web,   the

  reflection,   the lure of the world

    I love.

(BB 15–16)

The intensification of the play of sounds parallels the heightened apprehension of the poet—indicated typographically by the sign " • "
which demands a pause—his exhilarated discovery of the implications
of a poem that will never end. The falcon has felt "the lure of the
world" and "Passages" has found its stride.

The poet's apprehension is both exhilarating and fearful. The two
play off on another in "The Architecture: Passages 9," which weaves
together references to the poet's physical surroundings with passages
from Gustave Stickley's *Craftsman Homes* and an Indian legend published in Truman Michelson's *The Owl Sacred Pack of the Fox Indians.*
Moving easily from text to life and back, this poem exemplifies Duncan's ideal of being attentive to the poem when it appears, masterfully
presenting a domestic idyll of music and reading, suddenly threatened
by a much larger awareness.

The poem opens with a passage from Stickley describing an ideal
home, whose rooms must be recessed and broken up so that a "slight
feeling of mystery is given to it . . . when there is always something
around the corner." The attraction for Duncan of such tantalizing possibilities is apparent: not being able to see the whole room from any
one place is an analogue for not being able to see the entire field of
poetry from a single perspective.

The poet looks up from his book to see light falling from a recessed
window into his own room. The light's entry signifies an entry into
the field of the poem, into the "beyond." He then becomes aware of
"a little night music / after noon," but instead of Mozart he hears Kurt
Weill, and through him Brecht: "strains of *Mahagonny* on the phonograph / distant / intoxications of brazen crisis, / the (1930) *Können einem
toten Mann nicht helfen* chorus." As the chorus closes, the procession
"recesst," the stage darkens and he moves into another revery. A list of
books, called "keys," sends us back to the music but also evokes keys
to doors (passages) as well as mystery. Hesiod, Heraclitus, *The Zohar,
The Aurora,* each title has been an important book for Duncan, as "Pas-

sages" incorporates every aspect of the poet's life even as it sends the
reader to new areas of inquiry. The passages from Stickley emphasize
transitions, links, connections, while they are themselves disrupted.
Duncan's introduction described his attempts to transcend "our mere
human rationality": "Praise then the interruption of our composure,
the image that comes to fit we cannot account for, the juncture in the
music that appears discordant" (BB ix–x). Thus, instead of going up
the staircase, we go "below the house" and into "the dark" as the mystery mounts through us. Mounting carries its own mixed connotations
of transcendence and dominance, of spiritualization and sexual inter-
course, all associations of "the upper regions."

A larger "interruption of our composure" enters the poem with an
ominous command from "Owl": "*You are to make it.*" More book titles
follow (notably some children's tales), then an image of the poet lost
in a romance, and finally the explicit threat: "*You will often tell the story.
If you do that you will be able to marry those you love. You will fear me. If I
even see you, you will die.*" Without any intervening matter, the poem
closes with a line from Stickley finishing the earlier passage about the
staircase as a link to the upper regions of the house, "which belong to
the inner and individual part of the family life."

Why the threat? Duncan's sense of his own poetics includes an
awareness of the dangers involved. While the poem cannot and should
not be seen as entirely rational, it does suggest that the poet's role is
that of risk-taker, even in everyday life and domesticity. The poem
exemplifies the difficulties and dangers of the premise of incompleteness and of "these discords, these imperatives of the poem that exceed
our proprieties, these interferences" (BB x). A poem that can go on
forever is indeed threatening. Further, the "romance" calls forth imagery of adventure and danger. But most important, the association, if
only by juxtaposition, of such threatening demands with "the inner
and individual part of the family life" rings another change on the
relationship of the individual to others. The poem closes in the hypnagogic mode again; the poet is "lost" in his reading, lulled by the
revery of lamp, book, and music.

"The Fire: Passages 13" opens and closes with a list of thirty-six
words, arranged in rows and columns six by six. At the first level of
reading, they demand that the reader virtually chant them, pausing on
every word to allow it to do its work. Duncan says he had in mind "a
scene of early childhood, a dawn-of-man scene" (FC 32). This pattern

of words and the subsequent questions about "the old language" and "the old belief" link this poem with "Tribal Memories" in an invocation of high seriousness.

Etymologically, *matrix* means womb, and by extension a place of origin or growth. Duncan's awareness of this root is evident in the lines cited earlier from "In the Place of a Passage 22," "Grand Mother of Images, matrix / genetrix." Further, this matrix can be read in any order, just as, ideally, the entire set of "Passages" could be read as if it were a mobile, "each part as it is conceived as a member of every other part, having, as in a mobile, an interchange of roles, by the creation of forms within forms as we remember" (BB ix). At the end of the poem the matrix turns on its minor axis, revolving 180 degrees as if it were a three-dimensional mobile.

Three-dimensionality challenges a poet interested in disrupting conventions of linearity and spatiality, and so another level of significance arises. In addition to functioning as a chant, a genetrix, and a mobile, this matrix sends the reader to nuclear physics, for it evokes the matrices with which field physicists represent three-dimensional electron patterns in a two-dimensional mathematical grid. (Field physics is concerned with continuous functions in space and time, such as elasticity theory or hydrodynamics, in contrast to corpuscular physics' interest in the individual particle. The two are finally inseparable and cooperative, as I understand it).

The attempt to produce a literal picture of the atom as a miniature solar system, with electron particles orbiting the nucleus like planets, collapsed in the 1920s, when it became more common to think not of orbits but of energy levels. Electrons move from one energy level to another, emitting or absorbing quanta of energy in the process. In 1925, Werner Heisenberg designed a model showing energy levels of atoms in rectangular arrays or matrices of numbers, which could then be manipulated according to mathematical principles. No actual picture of the atom was required, and the model was not to be confused with the reality. In a similar model, Wolfgang Pauli's spin matrices explain his theory of the exclusion principle which accounts for a number of the properties of matter, notably the question of particles' occupying the same state without occupying the same point in space. Any matter can be considered to consist of a matrix of atoms held in position by the force of other atoms. The energies of such matrices form a field that demonstrates the properties of that matter, and Duncan's matrix explicitly abstracts the principles of field composition by breaking down syntax altogether in a visual representation of the energy field. Just as classical models of physical reality tended to carry connotative associations inappropriate to the reality, language is so charged with connotation that rock bottom is hard to attain, but Duncan's method here opens this poem with an asyntactic structure, charged with energy and meaning in infinite combinations, regardless of Duncan's awareness of Pauli or Heisenberg.[5]

I am not being disingenuous here. Duncan's eclectic erudition is legendary, and his interest in field physics is documented. He told George Bowering and Robert Hogg that Murray Gell-Mann's breakthrough in particle physics helped expand his notion of the universe and consequently of poetry: "Science is always advancing new pictures of what the universe is, . . . [so that] when you really had a massive conversion, . . . you have a conversion of form, entirely." Murray Gell-Mann, who named the elementary particles quarks, had a sense of humor (he took the name from *Finnegans Wake*), but also had an elegantly simple explanation of the heart of matter, a recent description of which illuminates the theory's appeal for a poet: "Physicists who are quite confident quarks exist nonetheless give odds that one will never be seen in isolation. . . . It is an invisible presence, all around us and even within us, and yet forever intangible; it has roughly the same status in physics as the soul has in theology."[6] Gell-Mann first announced his theory in 1964, the year of this "Passage." Whether Duncan knew it then or not, the interest in physics is there, and the multiple ramifications of the matrix that opens and strongly closes this poem are no less rich.

The next two lines, "blood disc / horizon flame," suggest "the cosmic energies fusing together into the spirit of creation."[7] Then the poet again appears to be gazing out his window in another hypnagogic revery, perhaps induced by the hypnotic pattern of the words above. After his questions about the old language, he turns to a description of Piero di Cosimo's remarkable landscape, *A Forest Fire*. The description is accurate but not detailed, focusing on the particulars of interest to the poet, notably that the predator/prey relationships break down ("lion and lamb lie down, quail / heed not the eagle") as do the divisions of species ("the man-Faced roe," "the wild boar too / turns a human face," [BB 41]). The poem comments upon the painting, particularly its "glow at the old borders" as Duncan's interest sharpens, and then relates the painting to the "magic" of Pletho, Ficino, Pico

Piero di Cosimo, *A Forest Fire* (1490–1500). Ashmolean Museum, Oxford. "We see at last the man-faced roe and his / gentle mate. . . . The ox / is fierce with terror, his thick tongue / slavers and sticks out panting / to make the gorgoneion face" ("The Fire: Passages 13").

della Mirandola, then to David's song and Orpheus's music, together
all comprising "chords and melodies of the spell that binds / the many
in conflict in contrasts of one mind." As the allusions multiply, major
themes of boundaries and junctions operate actively here. Limits form
and dissolve as the whole continually reconstitutes itself.

Di Cosimo's attractions for Duncan are clear from the most cursory
description of his art: he is an artist of many influences but his work
is not dominated by any one of them, Lionello Venturi tells us; rather,
"he is a painter who, defying classification, opened vistas on the future.
For he displays incomparable maestria in reconciling the facts of visual
experience with the fantastic inventions of his prolific imagination."
Further, his creative impulse is "based on an exceptional feeling for,
and understanding of, the archetypal myths of remote antiquity."
While his work was strikingly original and unorthodox, it seems "his
age lacked the spiritual maturity needed to sustain such splendid
gifts."[8]

The poem returns to a discussion of the painting, specifically com-
menting on di Cosimo's interrogation of boundaries, his pushing
against limits, long one of the major motifs of "Passages":

> Di Cosimo's   featherd, furrd, leafy
> boundaries where   even the Furies are birds
>   and blur   in higher harmonies Eumenides;
>   whose animals, entering a charmd field
> in the light of his vision, a stillness,
>   have their dreamy glades and pastures.
> The flames, the smoke.   The curious
>   sharp focus in a flow   sight
>   in the Anima Mundi has.

Any proposition immediately invites its opposite. Just as concord is
meaningless without discord, the Anima Mundi here is confronted by
the "*lascivia animi*" of modern life, through a contrast of di Cosimo's
painting with Bosch's *Christ Bearing the Cross,* in which "Hell breaks
out an opposing music," and a grotesque collection of the "faces of the
deluded" appears. Their leering and lewdness is symptomatic of the
lascivia animi of the modern world: "at last the faces of evil openly /
over us, / bestial extrusions no true animal face knows." In contrast to
di Cosimo's idyllic blurring of man and animal, the poet finds in the
Bosch neither animal nor human, but instead "a Devil's mimic of man,
a Devil's chemistry." Only Christ's face (and perhaps those of the good
thief and Veronica, though the poet does not mention them) "has an

Hieronymus Bosch, *Christ Bearing the Cross* (1505–10). Musee des Beaux-Arts, Ghent.
"About Him, as if to drown sweet music out, / Satan looks forth from / men's faces" ("The Fire: Passages 13").

echo in the stag's face we saw before." Satan looks forth from the faces of men, no longer the crucifiers in the Bosch, but those possessed to-day, by name. Even Duncan's lines are compressed, heightening the contrast with di Cosimo's spacious idyll:

> Eisenhower's idiot grin, Nixon's
> black jaw, the sly glare in Goldwater's eye, or
> the look of Stevenson lying in the U.N. that our
> Nation save face •

"Saving face" is an absolute wonder of irony and appropriateness in the context of these two paintings. Bosch's combination of pessimism and understanding of his fellowmen generated powerful visions for an ex-

cited time, when it was widely believed that the coming of the An-
tichrist and the end of the world were imminent. Duncan here
enumerates the scientists responsible for the "inevitable • at Los Ala-
mos," Oppenheimer, Fermi, Vannevar Bush, "plotting the holocaust
of Hiroshima • / Teller openly for the Anti-Christ." The magnitude of
our modern "fire" should not obscure our common human situation.

More than another *O tempora, O mores,* this poem also includes a
passage from Whitman's *Eighteenth Presidency,* a vigorous diatribe
against the absurdities of politics in 1856. The poem argues that such
evils are a constant of human experience, and confronts the ultimate
evil of which military and political events are simple manifestations. Yet
di Cosimo and Bosch were virtual contemporaries, and by "presenting"
them to us the poem makes them synchronous with us. In its Whit-
manic naming of the disorder, the poem evokes the larger order with
a confidence beyond the conscious knowledge of poet and reader. "I do
not know the old language," he confesses at the beginning of the poem,
yet surely it is here, beyond the boundaries of the poet's personal limits
and our own. As the poem firmly closes with the revolution of the
mobile of root words on its axis, we emerge from its spell with an
experience that cannot be rationally described. The introduction to
Bending the Bow comes fully to bear in "The Fire" in its contempt for
the "rationality" of war and its concern for boundaries ("It is a boundary beyond our understanding," [i]). With its wide-ranging allusiveness and its faithfulness to its principles of generation, "The Fire" fully
sets forth that "cross-section of the universe" which Whitehead calls
"presentational immediacy" and Duncan calls a "Passage."

The proposition of an entry into a larger field of awareness than that
of the individual carries with it a corollary belief in freedom within
law and individuality within community so that Duncan is more "con-
servative" than his readers of the 1960s may have thought. That con-
servatism was not immediately apparent to readers of such poems as
"The Multiversity: Passages 21" or *Of the War: Passages 22–27.* These
poems were both praised and attacked as overtly political, as if the
preceding poems had not been intimately concerned with the polis, the
City, and the place of the individual within larger orders. A reading of
"The Multiversity" shows these poems to be natural extensions of
"Passages."

One source of the bitterness with which the poem was attacked was
its statement that such manifestations of evil are "not men but heads
of the hydra," but as Duncan and others have noted, Chancellor Strong
is not the dragon but its victim. The scales of the dragon are "men

officized—ossified," dead to conscience and to inner law. As such, they propagate "false news"—locally, lying to undermine the Free Speech Movement, and nationally, "Stevenson, lying in the U.N. to save face" as in "The Fire."

Instead of falseness, the poem proposes the ideal City:

> Where there is no commune,
>   the individual volition has no ground.
> Where there is no individual freedom, the commune
>   is falsified.
>
> (BB 71)

These words, Duncan told the Rimer's Club in 1966, are from Vanzetti's condemnation of the Bolshevik regime in his insistence on a voluntary communism. The interconnectedness of all things and people informs the poetic sequence and its very manner of proceeding.

Thus ends and beginnings interchange, as in the passage near the end of this poem:

> Each day   the last day;   each day   the
>   beginning   the first word
>   door of the day or law awakening we create,
>   vowels sung in a field in mid-morning
>   awakening the heart from its oppressions.
>
> (BB 72)

Just as day revolves into night and back, so this wave too shall pass, and the moment of passage, like the boundary between day and night that calls forth hypnagogic reveries, is the focus of interest, since in Whitehead's terms, "The continuum is present in each actual entity, and each actual entity pervades the continuum" (PR 83). Such an awakening is achieved through the poem, with its apprehension that etymologically *Evil* derives from the will to overrule "the Law man's inner nature seeks." This poem closes strongly, with a repetition of Vanzetti's accusations.

"Vowels sung in a field in mid-morning" hardly seems an appropriate resolution to this poem, with its jarring accusations and pessimistic contention, but again we are instructed in "Orders" of the underlying harmony of all things, of the "concords of order in order, / a contrapuntal communion of all things." We hear Emerson again, and not

false confidence but *cum fide,* with full faith in ultimate truth and
beauty, coming finally to

> . . . a poetry
> having so much of beauty
> that in whose progressions   rage,
>   grief, dismay transported—but these
> are themselves transports of beauty!
>   (BB 78–79)

Continuing the propositions of the earlier poems and extending
them into new areas, the next five "Passages" appeared in *Tribunals* and
later in *Ground Work.* Of particular concern in "The Concert: Passages
31" is the idea of order physically embodied in the stars but which also
"*reigneth* in the spirit." Like a work of art and each of the "passages,"
the star operates at multiple levels, an individual star but also part of
larger orders, constellations and galaxies, yet "each being of the universe free to itself / having its own law." We are reminded that "all of
creation moves with / a music" (GW 12). Duncan again emphasizes
the poem as an energy construct or dance, ultimately beyond rational
analysis. That the poet is working out of bounds, beyond the limits of
understanding, recalls the epigraph from Julian. The manner of proceeding is specifically out of Olson's "Projective Verse,"[9] invoked directly here:

> It is the Star Betelgeuse, Alpha Orionis
> pouring its light within the depths,
>   a single note its sphere,   each
> "word"   a severd distinct thing,   Eternity
>   already gone up into   "MUST MUST MUST"
> the Poet, his heart urgent,
>   leaping beyond him, writes: "MOVE,
> INSTANTER, ON ANOTHER!"
>   (GW 12)

Olson's instructions have led to many strong yet different poems—
those of Dorn, Creeley, Duncan, and others. Possessed by the poem,
out of bounds and beyond himself, the poet becomes prophetic, "reveals what lurks in the heart / —prayers . . . song and especially ecstatic / speaking in tongues" (Duncan's ellipses). Shouting and leaping
on the table, he is open to the caustic remarks of "the scholar," a ra-

tionalist whose reason is divorced from feeling. A "severd distinct thing," the "isolated satyr" stammers, yet through his poetry he becomes part of a larger order like a star, even as his heart breaks and his blood pours forth. Duncan even incorporates the skepticism of the scholar, who is unnecessarily severe, severing himself. The poet, in recognizing his severed quality, realizes the urge to release, to unbind, to enter the field of the uneven at all risks.

Similar propositions appear in the later "Passages." "Passages: Empedoklean Reveries" proclaims music is "the wedding ground of Harmony and Discordia," and "They never cease their continuous exchange." The excerpt cited earlier from "Passages: JAMAIS" ("*Never* being the name of what is infinite," we are told in "Empedoklean Reveries") repudiating reason in favor of "the Intention of a Universe" is of course a primary proposition of "Passages." That poem explicitly contrasts "God's Art, the principle of recognition" with "Man's art an other arbitration of the Whole." While individual "Passages" may appear to be fragmentary, poet and reader must yield to that impulse toward pattern that will allow them to glimpse the design.

This accounting of "Passages" is hardly definitive, for—besides being impossible—that would violate the proposition of the poem. Rather than being frustrating, however, such inconclusiveness opens an ever-widening area of activity. The inconclusion is indeed momentous, in yet another of Duncan's puns. It is important, and it is of the present moment, the passage of the here and now whose conclusion is death. The poem presents "no composure but a life-spring of dissatisfaction" (BB x), but this poem repays the attention it exacts.

Chimeras, Falconress, and Epilogos

Duncan's translation of Gerard de Nerval's *Chimeras* reflects his continuing strong interest in the occult in poetry. Although somewhat condescending in its treatment of Robin Blaser's versions of these same poems, his lengthy discussion in *Audit* 4, no. 3, of these poems' importance to him and of his feeling *called* to translate them is informative and demonstrates the lures Nerval's poetry held for him: "From Darwin I had come to see all contemporary living things—man and elephant, fish and bird—as creative forms of soul and spirit, created in a process of evolution that so surpassed the bounds of brain thinking that it seemed to us to be Chance and without will or design" (46). Duncan's concern with the appearance of his published work, which some might

regard as fastidious, also has a key chapter of its history in this
quence. The poems originally appeared in *Audit,* but in the first edi
tion of the book by New Directions an entire page was omitted, with
the pages apparently renumbered by the printer to conceal the error.
(Duncan explains what happened in *Caterpillar* 7 [April 1969]:89–91).

"My Mother Would Be a Falconress" (52–54), which Duncan has
called one of the fastest poems he ever wrote, presents a good example
of the tone leading of vowels, a dance of alliterative music. His introductory sketch, "A Lammas Tiding," reports that "the troubled insistence of the lines would not let go of me" (51), and the troubling
dream the poem recounts attests to the poet's honesty. Duncan hu-
morously reports that he thought of himself as a peaceful chicken rather
than a ravenous hawk: "Which goes to show one should be careful of
vain self-delusions entertaind at bedtime" (51).

The poem presents Duncan as the falcon mastered by his mother.
Their relationship is intricately bound up in the central themes of obedience and freedom, the setting of limits versus a flight beyond the
horizon, love and terror. The play of such opposites generates the field
of this anguished poem. An examination of the first, middle, and final
stanzas will allow at least some sense of the interplaying rime of sound
and theme:

My mother would be a faconress,
And I, her gay falcon treading her wrist,
would fly to bring back
from the blue of the sky to her, bleeding, a prize,
where I dream in my little hood with many bells
jangling when I'd turn my head.
. . . .
I tear at her wrist with my beak to draw blood,
and her eye holds me, anguisht, terrifying.
She draws a limit to my flight.
Never beyond my sight, she says.
She trains me to fetch and to limit myself in fetching.
She rewards me with meat for my dinner.
But I must never eat what she sends me to bring her.

. . . .
My mother would be a faconress,
and even now, years after this,
when the wounds I left her had surely heald,
and the woman is dead,

> her fierce eyes closed, and if her heart
> were broken, it is stilld •
>
> I would be a falcon and go free.
> I tread her wrist and wear the hood,
> talking to myself, and would draw blood.

Note the modulation of vowels in the final lines' "would," "tread," "hood," "would" again, and "blood"; of "head" and "hood"; of "falconress" with "treading her wrist" in the first stanza and with "years after this" in the last. The insistent long *i*s of the opening stanza—"My," "I," "fly," "sky" and "prize"—serve to emphasize the key words and, at the same time, to play off the other long vowel set, "be," "bleeding," and "dream." The fact that such effects work subliminally for most readers until they are pointed out does not undercut Duncan's theory of "the tone leading of vowels": "An initial tone once sounded carries over in the mind as a bass tone thru out the time of the poem. Much of the pleasure of the poem lies in the echoes and reiterations of this sound—that forms a chord of memory—giving a satisfaction equal to that of the masterly and beautiful end rhyme, the jewel, as conservatives justly protest, of poetic achievement."[10]

Further, the unusual syntax, which makes some of the modifiers ambiguous ("bleeding" in line four, "anguisht, terrifying" in the middle stanza), is both intentional and significant, as is the dot appearing in the final stanza. According to Duncan's introduction, "The immediate event—the phrase within its line, the adjoining pulse in silence, the new phrase—each part is a thing in itself; the junctures not binding but freeing the elements of configuration so that they participate in more than one figure [much like whole poems from Passages, as we have seen]. A sign appears—"•"—a beat syncopating the time at rest; as if there were a stress in silence. He strives not for a disintegration of syntax but a complication within syntax, overlapping structures, so that words are freed, having bounds out of bound" (ix). Even a poem as personal as this one, a transcription of a dream, fulfills the large demands he makes of a poem, the full articulation of which is itself beyond the bounds of our ability to measure it.

The book's final poem, "Epilogos" (134–37) is a moving love poem and a series of four "takes" on some lines from "Doves," a poem in *Roots and Branches* that Duncan wrote in response to the news that H. D. had suffered a stroke that crippled her speech. Each take is a meditation on speech and poetry, from the moan of grief and of love

to the transparent speech of true poetry once the poet surrenders his
own will to that of the poem. Facing the limits of language, the
"sounds and compounds of sounds men define / and pronounce differently riming," the first take asks, "how is one / to speak making speech
with such utterings?" While the first take's metaphor is the tree of the
universe, "forcing out of us a statement, a green bud, / where creation
that's a tree / must speak as it can," the second take's metaphor is a
cup. Risking "certain uncertainties" in his poem and in his relationship
with his beloved, the poet finds that "Brimfull / the cup my heart is
upon the very / edge / of spilling its more than can be contain'd, its /
happening so / in what is happening." In the third take, "speech comes
back to where it left off," and the poet at first resists the ache of need
and "the rime wont come thru or I wont / accept the word '*moan*.'"
Recognition of the rime is followed by its acceptance: "I'll / take whatever words for it that fit," leading to the final take's direct self-description, in an appropriately inconclusive conclusion to the book:

> I am a man of words, a
> man of my word. I get the drift I do not
> know. The Word moves me. I give in to it.
> I give into it my will, into it
> the intent of the poem.

Chapter Eight
Ground Work: Before the War (1984)

On 11 December 1971 Duncan wrote to Jonathan Williams about his new book, *Ground Work*: "Let the *Field, Roots,* and the *Bow* stand for whatever publicity I'm to have. I've not had anything like the good Abbe Liszt's public career, but his 'it seems to me, now, high time that I should be forgotten' appeals to me for my own intentions in work. *Ground Work* is an effort, slow in getting under weigh, to move into a dimension where new work will take place more and more in the dimension of a private world."[1] With a public announcement in the preface to *Caesar's Gate* the following year, Duncan took the astonishing step of refusing to publish a major book of poetry until 1984. The poems in *Volume One* were written largely between 1968 and 1975, with work since then scheduled to appear in *Ground Work, Volume Two: In the Dark* in 1989, the poet's seventieth year.

In an age of media consciousness, mass appeal, and self-promotion even among poets, Duncan's gesture was regarded as suicidal for his reputation. Indeed, what reputation he had seems to have been eclipsed—*Ground Work* went virtually unnoticed in the national media (the *New York Times Book Review* did give it half of page thirteen), and Duncan, never popular among anthologists, has been omitted from Helen Vendler's recent canonization of contemporary American poets. Incredibly, M. L. Rosenthal and Sally Gall even managed to exclude Duncan from their recent study, *The Modern Poetic Sequence,* to that book's lasting damage.[2] Admittedly, Duncan is getting what he asked for, and he has refused to allow his work to be included in many anthologies. Nonetheless, to protest such neglect some three hundred fellow poets created the National Poetry Award and awarded it to him.

The unusually wide format of *Ground Work,* presenting a photocopy of Duncan's typescript without an intervening typesetter, presents further evidence of Duncan's displeasure with the commercial publishing process.[3] Lines are permitted to extend to their full length, and white

spaces are generous. Duncan had considered such a format as early as
The Opening of the Field, but the fiasco of the omission of one full poem
and part of another from *Bending the Bow* and the printer's deliberate
cover-up confirmed his decision. Andrew Schelling cleverly relates
Duncan's insistence on exactness to Dante's elaborate terza rima measures—in both cases, any alteration or forgery is prevented.[4] As Duncan's preface, "Some Notes on Notation," explains, his typewriter
spacing corresponds with his composition, so that all aspects of the
poem's appearance—caesuras, line breaks, spacings, stanza breaks, internal margins—must be attended to. "All 'typographical' features are
notations for the performance of the reading. Margins signify" (n.p.).
The preface explains his notations, even to so simple and important a
matter as indicating whether a page break involves a stanza break. The
explanations are deft and precise, but to need them at this late date,
after Cummings, Williams, Pound, and Olson, is a sad commentary
on the attention poetry receives. Duncan's preface alerts us to the ca-
dence and the dance of his form, to the "sounded silence" as an integral
element, to what he calls in "Passages 33" "the line / / a trial, each
element a crisis of attention" (22). Perhaps that insistence on attention
is the reason Duncan has resigned himself to writing for a relatively
small audience.

The book's title proposes a return to elemental work, a poetry that
must continually prepare for new work. Duncan told Ronald Johnson
that the subtitle should be read as in "before a mirror," and Schelling
notes that "in the apocalypse that History enacts, *before* sheds its temporal implication." In a world whose language has been corrupted by
governments, multinational corporations, and the media, "Responsible
users of language, those who Robert Duncan says have maintained 'the
ability to respond,' stand as never before 'Before the War.' Words in
this Era of Information manifest themselves as monstrously efficient
instruments of domination and deceit. . . . When the war 'comes
home' to brain and larynx, and to the space between all of us, Poetry—
writing writ large *or* small—becomes a mapping of worlds in which
both world and map are inextricably at stake."[5]

Ground Work, then, is both a continuation and a movement away
from Duncan's earlier work. Major themes continue, as do the sets
"Passages" and "The Structure of Rime." His active use of his deriva-
tions is evident not only in "A Seventeenth Century Suite" and "Dante
Études" but in other poems' allusions to Paul Celan, Denise Levertov,
Pound, Stevens, Thom Gunn, Heraclitus and Jalāl al-Dīn Rūmī;

"Transmissions: Passages 33" presents itself explicitly as "this art an aggregate of intentions," alluding to Brancusi, John Adams, Scriabin, Wagner, Swinburne, Creeley, Pound, Pythagoras, Tirgu-Jui, cubism, Corbusier, Leger, Mondrian, De Stijl, Moreau, Oedipus, Odysseus, and Whitman. Noting that thematically *Ground Work* extends from *Bending the Bow,* Michael Davidson finds it closer to *Roots and Branches* in its "high romantic diction and neoplatonic subjects."[6] The book presents a break as well, however, for as Thomas Parkinson has observed, unlike the other three major volumes, "*Ground Work* does not so insistently stick or hang together" as a book. Rather, "the inclusive book *Ground Work* collects collections and composes an aggregate or conglomerate."[7] While Duncan attempts to avoid overcomposition, then, this book even in its movement away from earlier work is an outgrowth of that work.

The first and last poems, for instance, sound continuing themes and bracket the book's other poems. "Achilles' Song," dated 10 December 1968, emphasizes the poet's working beyond his conscious knowledge. The Muse in the form of the Sea presents him with "waves of meaning" which have a "sounding and resounding power." Such a muse is a figure of the mother but also of dread, its "shoreless depth" and "crumbling shores" promising both ecstasy and dissolution. The turning and returning tides are likewise figures for the lines of the poem, "words turnd in the phrases of song / before our song."

The final poem, "Circulations of the Song after Jalāl al-Dīn Rūmī," likewise opens with the poet's not knowing and his heart leaping forward "past knowing." This poem about his own art and his love for Jess, in addition to returning to the recurring theme of love and poetry, is aptly modeled on the work of Rūmī, a thirteenth century Persian mystic who also attributed his poetry to his beloved. Rūmī's dithyrambic lyrics recall Duncan's interest in the dithyramb as early as *The Venice Poem.* Indeed, Rūmī's disciples, known in the west as the Whirling Dervishes, sought ecstasy through an elaborate dancing ritual, just as the rhythms of both poets invite us to partake in the dance. Duncan's lines explicitly celebrate the mystic union attainable through love and art:

> I am like a line cast out
>> into a melodic unfolding beyond itself
>> a mind hovering ecstatic
> above a mouth in which the heart rises

> pouring itself into liquid and fiery speech
> for the sake of a rime not yet arrived
>   containing again and again resonant arrivals.
>   (168)

Incorporated into this poem are such Duncan hallmarks as puns (court, courtesy; rest [pause], rest [remainder]); allusions to Shakespeare, Emerson, Hermes, and Pound; and tone-leading vowels. The latter are quite evident, for instance, in the book's concluding sixteen lines, which eloquently bring home both literally and figuratively the characteristic Duncan motif: that the emblem of both love and poetry must be constancy in incessant change.

Ground Work offers many remarkable individual poems. "A Song from the Structures of Rime Ringing as the Poet Paul Celan Sings" (8) displays intense wordplay, especially on "something" and "nothing," and describes itself in the line "It is totally untranslatable." "Despair in Being Tedious" (9), the final poem of *Caesar's Gate,* effectively closed that book with references to "Great Asia beyond the horizon," with incessant Prufrockian self-interrogation, and with a disarming awareness of the poet's "manic spiel of wheel in wheel," which drives away his listeners. "Childhood's Retreat" (49), a reminiscence of a secret hideaway "in the perilous boughs of the tree," presents an autobiographical experience as a universal truth in the fearful climb "into the shaking uncertainties" of adulthood.

The "grand architecture that the Muses command" unfolds in "The Museum" (59–61), another confrontation with a Jungian *anima,* at once "the figure of a womanly grace" and "the Bestial Muse, the devouring *Impératrice.*" Proposing again the pun on amusement and what a Muse meant, the poem recapitulates the poet's passage "from fear into a radiance," "the vision of this very art in which, out of no confidence, their confidential song comes into me." Despite his awareness of the Jungian *anima's* presence in this poem, "a protesting of all that feminine potentially in me against my dominating personality" as well as his own "distaste for what Anaïs Nin and M. L. Rosenthal saw in me and found repulsive," Duncan told Abbott and Shurin that "Jung's archetypes can't possibly account for the event that people have. It's always unique. Each poet is needed somehow. . . . [W]e search thru poetry for the uniqueness to be found there, not just a repetition of an event & certainly not for an archetype" (*Sunshine* 4, and *Soup* 33).

Finally, the memorable "Bring It up from the Dark" (53) presents briefly the pervasive theme of Duncan's "poetics of responsibility," to use Jed Rasula's good phrase. Unlike many protesters against the war in Viet Nam, Duncan confronts the "news from beyond the horizon" as a personal responsibility, fully recognizing his own implication: "Men of our own country / send deadly messengers we would not send," so that "now wraiths / of the dead men daily they kill rise / against us." Rasula laments the painful state of much recent American poetry, which merely competes with television, radio, and video arcades for leisure time. "What can leisure time be," Rasula asks, "when our political condition is Standby Alert? What is poetry doing by competing for leisure time, but vacating all ethical premises? Robert Duncan has spent 20 years reminding us that the evil we see elsewhere is something that imaginative strengths permit us to see in ourselves."[8] Looking back to "Passages 35" and ahead to "'*A pretty Babe*'—that burning Babe," "Bring It up from the Dark" fulfills the poet's responsibilities in all their anguish: "Dream disclosed to me, I too am Ishmael."

Sets of Poems

As Parkinson noted above, at least in part *Ground Work* collects collections. The book contains ten "Passages," including the five previously published as *Tribunals,* and three from "The Structure of Rime," two sets of poems dealt with at length in the previous chapter. Four additional sets appear here also. The "Santa Cruz Propositions" fully embrace the anima, while juxtaposing newspaper accounts of a grisly murder in the Santa Cruz mountains, Socrates' theory of love, and Duncan's reactions to Denise Levertov's increasingly strident antiwar poetry. The first poem presents the poet as a would-be surfer frustrated by the inevitable breaking of the wave. Poetry, which can be "a torrent of confidence beyond thought," invariably "withdraws its promise" and plummets the poet into "the *cold* of the sea." Variably named "Old Mama Mammemory," "Old Mummummymurmurur," "the shadowy Big Presence of her," "the Dumb Waitress," and "Woman of Water," the indifferent Muse is both needed and not needed, wanted and not wanted. "The Muse consumes utterly," indifferent to the fascinated boy playing with his blocks (recalling "Passages 6: The Collage") under her wing:

> There is no dream in which the high throne
>   of the poet's personal Empire does not finally come
>   to the dark shore of *Her* flood
> and his word-power go out futilely
> to war with the insolent mob where
>   her boundaries advance.
>
> (38)

The poet's imperialism pales at such dark shores, at a flood without a covenant and rainbow. Nonetheless, this poem concludes, this Mother and the Ur-Father generate a fecund strife, "from which the consonances and dissonances of lives vibrate."

The second poem introduces the interwoven narratives of the gruesome Santa Cruz murder and of that part of Plato's *Symposium* which recounts Socrates' instruction in the metaphysic of love by his teacher, Diotima of Mantinea. Ironic as these juxtapositions prove to be, the entire poem is framed in a cosmic struggle of male and female forces, with a male protagonist entwined in the net of a feminine Fate who calls "Soccer Tease" her saint, because "with an assumed knowingness about his / gnawing Nothing so that he wants Knot / that has befuddled Philosophy with method. / Him and his nosey sayauton!" (40). The final phrase's harsh attack on Socrates' cornerstone, *gnothi seauton* (know thyself), echoes through the rest of the poem's account of the murderer's search for reality and the dialogue on love. Alcibiades the Tyrant, alluded to in this poem, called Socrates a satyr and a bully even in the course of praising his virtues, so that this complex and highly allusive poem is not a clear-cut discussion of good and evil, but rather a stressful confrontation with the fruitful agonies and ecstasies of both love and self-knowledge.

The final poem, then, only seems to break away sharply when it turns to Denise Levertov and her poetry. Duncan had been a friend of hers for years, but he was deeply disturbed by her vehement reaction to the war in Viet Nam, seeing her behavior as self-destructive and projecting her as Kali, the goddess of destruction. This poem is part of a phenomenal public exchange that includes several other poems in this book, since it incorporates several of her poems (most notably "The Year One," "Ghandi's Gun" and "I Thirst" from *To Stay Alive,* 1971), and since in return it is answered by her in such poems as "Part II" and "Report," also in that volume.[9] Quite apart from the powerful dynamics of this interaction of two of our finest poets, no mere sum-mary can recapture this complex sequence's unblinking gaze into the terror at the eye of the storm, into the impossible choice between Plato's "Love as Need" and Levertov's "Love as Anger."

Six poems with homosexual themes are collected as "Poems from the Margins of Thom Gunn's *Moly,*" most directly derived from Gunn's brief citation of the passage in the *Odyssey* in which Hermes gives Odysseus moly, the plant which protects him against Circe, and from Gunn's first two poems from *Moly* (1973), "Rites of Passage" and "Moly."[10] Though Gunn's work is characterized by regular stanzas and tight rime schemes, Duncan has found strong thematic affinities in Gunn, most particularly in the interrogation of margins (note Duncan's title), especially those that indicate the limits or the identity of the self, what Gunn calls in "Being Born," the memory "of man and boundary blended" (Gunn 38). While any number of Gunn's poems explore the loss of transcendence of self (e.g., "Tom-Dobbin," "The Color-Machine," "The Discovery of the Pacific," "Street Song," "The Fair in the Woods"), his poems from the *Odyssey* draw on the classic episode in which Circe transforms Odysseus's men into swine. His "Rites of Passage" and "Moly" are both spoken by one of the transformed sailors, whose thoughts Homer does not give us. Gunn's speaker describes the transformation in "Rites of Passage" in threatening, directly Oedipal terms; in "Moly," he awakens to his "nightmare of beasthood," his manhood "buried in swine" as he desperately searches for the moly: "From this fat dungeon I could rise to skin / And human title, putting pig within" (Gunn 7).

Duncan, characteristically, injects some torque into his derivations. His first two poems, comprising a "Preface to the Suite," set the terms by recalling the transitions of adolescence, the aching anguish of being between childhood and adulthood:

> Childhood, boyhood, young manhood
> ached at the heart with it,   the unnameable,
> the incompletion of desires,   and at the margins
> shook.
>
> (GW 63)

Now, half a century later, the poet recalls the season of his adolescence, straining at "the margins of my thought."

Trying to recall the "ghosts and lovers of my sixteenth year," the poet struggles to remember "the fathering dream," and the final stanza of the second poem confronts his memories of that time and of his stepfather's death in a dizzying rush of wordplay and internal rime and off-rime not a whit less brilliant for being irregular:

> The year my father died died into me and dyed
> anew the green of green, the gold gold shone from,
> the blue that colors seas and skies to speak
> of sadness innocence most knew, and into Man
> a mystery to take the place of fatherhood he grew
> in me, a ghostly bridegroom fathering his bride in me,
> an emptiness in which an absence I call *You*
> was present, a pride, a bright unanswering bliss,
> consumed my heart. It was a fiery ghost,
> a burning substitution darkening all the sexual ways,
> striving in those urgencies to speak, to speak,
> to heal unutterable injuries. It was a wounded mouth,
> a stricken thing unable to release its word,
> a panic spring no youthful coming could exhaust in me.
>
>   (GW 64)

This dark dream of dying out of childhood into sexual awakening resonates with rimes of content (father and bridegroom, innocent sadness and unanswering bliss, absence and presence, darkness and fire) and of sound—note only the first and eighth lines, and the reinforcing rime of "a stricken thing" and "a panic spring" in the final two lines.

In the Moly suite itself, "Near Circe's House" presents the tale from Hermes' viewpoint, as the "eternal and self-contain'd" god offers his aid to Odysseus in a telling pun: "Take my heart from me / and it will beat for you, wildly," and "take heart from me." "Rites of Passage: I," "Moly," and "Rites of Passage: II" complete the suite with a dual focus on transformation as transubstantiation and on the measures of poetry, united in Duncan's play on metrical feet and feet changed into hooves. The poems interweave their joint themes of change, especially sexual awakening, and expression:

> A hearing stiffens, strains at the leash of a wild dancing.
> As if answering an as-yet-unspoken need,
> upon the brow of a silence behind my words
> the pensive horns of a new yearning thrust.

> The force of a rime impending runs abroad,
> forebodings at the edge we are in ourselves.
>
> (67)

Once again, both love and poetry force us to the limits of ourselves and beyond, to apprehensions that are both enthralling and fearful. Even as Circe transforms men into beasts, the soaring dance of poetry can quickly go "down into the throat, / gagging" the poet who is "snared in a / delirium of snout and watering mouth / incapable of speech." Most telling and most fearful is the recognition that these forms arise from the inner self. Gunn's speaker is shocked by "what germs, what jostling mobs there were in me" (Gunn 6), just as Duncan admits that the "Dear Beast, dear dumb illiterate / Underbeing of Man" waits "in the depths of / my sleeping self, . . . / . . . in the mind my mind / verges upon" (GW 68).

Duncan's use of sources takes on a new dimension with "A Seventeenth Century Suite in Homage to the Metaphysical Genius in English Poetry (1590–1690)," an eleven-poem series that reprints entire poems by Walter Raleigh, Robert Southwell, George Herbert, and John Norris of Bemerton, as well as some forty lines from a 947-line masque by Ben Jonson; these are followed by, in the words of Duncan's subtitle for the suite, "Imitations, Derivations & Variations upon Certain Conceits and Findings Made among Strong Lines."

Duncan's sixth and seventh poems (76–79), after Herbert's "Jordan I" and "Jordan II," follow Herbert's plea for plainness in poetry, as opposed to the intricacies of the popular poetry of his time. Though this may at first strike the reader as patent irony, Duncan is serious in his call for a poetry with the truth of "immediate life" and against the "serpent-wise word-twistings, / the artist's marquetry, fashiond in cunning, / tail turnd on tail to convey the torque / that style demands" (77). As Herbert's "Jordan I" clarifies, both poets are also admonishing that part of themselves that loves ornamentation and the display of one's abilities. Just as the poem's close attention to sound and rhythm recalls both the Metaphysical poets and Duncan's earlier work, Duncan's lines relate his poetics clearly:

> If we but trust the song I know
>   its course is free
> and straight and steady goes to work its good;
>   it needs but trust unquestioning.
>
> (79)

Likewise, Duncan's "Coda" (91–93), a final poem after Bemerton's "Hymne to Darkness," speaks of his confidence "beyond my knowing" in a poetry that derives "out of boundless Source seeking its bounds":

> *Our Father Who Art in Heaven* . . . I begin
> my prayer before the Night, and, gazing in,
> I wonder at the depth that I call *"Him"*.
> For *Heaven* is not that Spring of Lights
> that burns for Heaven's sake but darkens
>   into an emptying of sight.
>
>   (92)

Just as the resonance of "before the Night" instructs us how to read the subtitle of this book, the recognition of "The joy of an overtaking darkness" anticipates the subtitle of Volume Two, "in the dark." Paradoxically, vision requires "an emptying of sight," just as, in the poem's closing lines, "into the infancy of a darkening bliss / / Love sets me free." From their conceits and strong lines to their metaphysical beliefs, these poets present Duncan with a rich harvest.

Where Walter Raleigh presents life in the extended metaphor of a play, Duncan updates the metaphor to film, asking a very different question from Raleigh's "What Is Our Life?": "What does this life most seem?" In an apt wordplay, life seems to be "the event of a momentary sequence / that depended upon a place it had in common / among commonplaces." As if watching a film, "in the dark, the spectral spectator of all / expects a tragic loss in what we find and knows / the essential comedy when we fall" (71). In this both literally and figuratively dark vision, the poem asserts, "In death alone we are sincere. / We'll not return to take our bows or read reviews" (72), as Duncan explicitly takes his leave of fame and literary critics.

Quite apart from its congenial themes, Ben Jonson's *Hymenai: or The Solemnities of Masque, and Barriers* must have piqued Duncan's interest as soon as he noticed the masque honored the wedding of the Earl of Essex to Lady Francis Howard and that it was printed by Valentine Symmes. Not only was Howard his given middle name and Symmes his adopted surname, but Mr. Sims spelled his name differently and Duncan's altering the spelling in his own note serves to emphasize the point. In Jonson's masque, personified Truth and Opinion cannot be distinguished by their appearance, and their conflict is presented as a literal battle interrupted by an angel whose speech Duncan cites.

Duncan's poem in response is important because of its self-consciousness of its own grand, rhetorical manner, interrupting its own dance of soul (anima) and animal, its own "serpent-wise" wisdom that "writhes wise to a secret we fear":

> *"Her right hand holds a sun with burning rays"*
> —O.K. The mode's rhetorical. The manner, grand.
> And we've been commanded to put such childish things away.

The poem is a direct response to Ezra Pound's command to "strive for the essential, or make it new." Duncan lets his Muse revive "emotional enormities, old ways, grand ways, in me" (87). Accurately describing the "modern" stance he would prefer, he refuses to deny the other that calls him:

> But there she stands! as she is, insistent,
> In court dress, elaborately personified,
> decorate with *impresae* and symbolic fuss.
> And everywhere, the language is too much.
>   (88)

After citing four of Jonson's lush lines, he coyly laments, "Now what am I to do with that?" The reader can almost see Duncan's devilish grin as he proceeds through Jonson's "flowering confusion" to the lines that most directly answer Pound in his own terms, "Moving and yet still / she divides and multiplies my sense of her anew," stirring and combining "contrary tempers" in an "Eternall Unitie."

While Duncan may be avoiding fame and large audiences, his poetry returns often to public issues, and in three of the strongest poems of "A Seventeenth Century Suite" the war personified in Jonson's masque turns literal. "Passages 36" admits, "I know but part of it and that but distantly, / a catastrophe in another place, another time" (80–83), yet Duncan refuses to avoid his personal responsibility, here specifically for Viet Nam and Bangladesh, and "now" specifically 16 December 1971. In another poem with Denise Levertov clearly in mind, Platonic idealism offers no refuge ("Terror erodes its own events, / shadows having no more touch in time / than shadows, yet / there's no relief from that knowledge"), because "the ritual mutilation" is taking place "with hatred," yes, but even worse, "no longer having a feeling of what is done, / without hatred" as well. The carnage breeds not only physical but spiritual desolation, for "They move to destroy the sources of feeling." The war undermines poetry itself, by corrupting the language and by deadening all feeling. Rather than shifting blame to external causes, the poem concludes by returning to its opening lines, then confronting the poet's recollection of an argument with a friend (Levertov, I believe) and his conflict with his mother, finally closing in a moving confession of his own arrogance and intolerance. Personal failure parallels cosmic strife, in an inescapable conflict that simultaneously generates and destroys.

Finally, two poems in response to Robert Southwell's unusual Christmas poem, "The Burning Babe," strongly bring home Duncan's "poetics of responsibility." Also influenced by Denise Levertov's "Advent 1966," Duncan's poem doubles Southwell's vision. The first poem presents the Christ child, "alive with flame," but immediately the poet castigates his own refusal "to burn," to respond to Christ's passion. Rather, his burning is only "black jealousy," not living fire but ashes, "without Truth's heat / a cold of utter Winter that refused the Sun," in another accurate pun. The poem's close is a prayer, that what "is no more than an image in Poetry" might become actual, that the return of feeling might "undo" him, so that he may mysteriously be united with "the Language of What Is."

The second poem can be read as the fulfillment of that prayer, for feeling returns, and hotly. The second vision is a horror. Despite the martyr's comfort of the first vision, now he sees victims of napalm, babies that are literally on fire in the battlefields of Viet Nam, the "burnd faces / that have known catastrophe incommensurate / with meaning, beyond hate or loss or / Christian martyrdom." "I cannot imagine, gazing upon photographs / of these young girls," the poem continues, "the mind / transcending what's been done to them" (GW 75).

"The broild flesh of these heretics, / by napalm monstrously baptized" haunts the poet, whose vision recalls not Christmas but Good Friday: "Victor and victim know not what they do / —the deed exceeding what we would *know*." To escape responsibility would be to lose the ability to respond, however. "Our nation's store of crimes long / unacknowledged, unrepented" can no longer be ignored. The poet's greatest fear, in an effective dance of vowels, is that he will fail to feel, cringing from "the knowledge of what no man / can compensate. I think I could bear it. / / I cannot think I could bear it." When the victim is sacrificed not for us but by us, we inflict our own "catastrophe incommensurate / with meaning" upon ourselves.

Though the Dante Études (94–134) were written in the early seventies, simultaneously with "A Seventeenth Century Suite," Duncan proposes here a different kind of set. His brief preface calls attention to the musical analogy: "Dante 'études' rather than 'studies' because they are proposed in poetry as the études of Romantic composers were proposed in music, for I mean a music not a scholarly dissertation. Dante as Schumann in his humors might have overheard his meaning" (94). Though the poems are drawn from Duncan's reading of Dante's prose, attention to the immediate moment of his experience produces the poem: "I draw my 'own' thought in reading Dante as from a wellspring."

In a reading of the Études at Jack Shoemaker's house in Berkeley on 1 November 1974,[11] Duncan made some careful distinctions. Admitting that all his work since *Bending the Bow* had been "essentially interrupted forms," Duncan continued: "However, these are proposed as études in sets and not as études in sequences. This is *not* a suite like the 'Seventeenth Century Suite,' and I was struck by certain sets of Schumann's, for instance, where there's great doubt about whether they should be played entire under their opus number and certainly doubt about whether there's any significance in their being played in sequence, and I wanted a balance between the two." The poems were not, therefore, written in the order proposed, and resemble in some ways "Passages" and "The Structure of Rime." "I seem never to have conveyed the point that 'Structure of Rime' and 'Passages' are not long poems like *Maximus* or *The Cantos* and so forth. They belong in the volumes they appear, and they are actually sets of poems in études. Period. They have no such propositions about being great grand long poems. They are returns to a set. They belong to the set they're in, but that is not primary. They belong and even rime with poems surrounding them," as we have seen. "Yet there is a stream of consciousness and there is a chronology, . . . and now I can get wonderfully mixed up." Taking up roughly half the poems, out of sequence, will enable us to come to at least one level of understanding this complex set.

The Études' formal propositions are secondary to their insistence on Dante's immediate presence in the world of poetry. These meditations on the social and poetic order are drawn from Dante's discussions of *principium, civitas,* and *monarchia,* but, Duncan's preface tells us, Dante's mind "is not a mind researcht in the lore of another time, for me, but immediate, everlastingly immediate, to the presence of the idea of Poetry." Thus "On Obedience," the seventh poem of book 2, speaks of the freedom in obedience necessary to both love and poetry, derived here from *Il Convivio* yet certainly a recurring theme in Duncan's work:

> It must be
> completely under command,   not
> self-moved (these études,
> like Dante's odes,
> having their own ease
> I feel   and rule   that understanding
> I've but to follow thru,   do
> what their evolving likeness will
> prove in me, engrosst
> in every freedom allowd,   draw close)
>
> and measured,
> not out of measure;   the words proposed
>   to the edge of meaning
> and not beyond it, justified.

(118-19)

This poem and the two following poems directly address the reader in a convivial embrace, a living together in poetry ("And these studies demanded of me / that in my writing every reader / be *their* friend, / even as I, in writing, *theirs*," 120), even to becoming lovers: "O Lovers, I am only one of you! / We, convivial in what is ours!" (120). Duncan's persistent themes—the surrender of the ego, the transgression of boundaries, the freedom that is only found in obedience to larger orders—become still more insistent in their demands of both poet and reader, now springing from the work of a thirteenth-century Italian Catholic and exile, yet no less immediate for that.

The first two poems of book 1 set up the set in terms of our responsibility to language itself. "We Will Endeavor" (95–96) opens with Dante's commitment "to be of service / to the vernacular speech," in Duncan's fancy rooted in the "endearments" and "whisperings" of infancy. Recalling the "hermetic talk" of his own youth, Duncan presents the language as an integral part of the infant's experience of the world as Nurse, "out of hunger, instinctual / craving, thirst for 'knowing,' /

/ toward oracular teats." The measures of poetry are grounded in animal rhythms:

> lungs sucking-in the air, having
> heart in it, rhythmic; and,
>   moving in measure,
> self-creating in concert

—and therein,

noble.

"Professional, not noble," in contrast, is the concern with syntax, spelling, the "learned, / reflective, particular," as described in "Secondary is the Grammar" (96–98). Instead of trying "to mediate the immediate," the poet must master τέχνη, the "artfulness, steady and careful," that takes risks for "a felt architectonics then of the numinous," which nonetheless requires "expenditure of much time / and assiduous study." The return of "the old oracular voice" takes over "the poet's intention" and shames those "masters of grammar / who have denied their illiterate nurses."

Such an untraditional inclusiveness of animal ways of knowing enlarges the scope of "A Little Language" (98–99), at first reading an apparently slight vignette of the poet talking with his cat. No mere sentimentalizing of the pet, the poem insists that whales and wolves "know harmony and have an eloquence that stirs / my mind and heart—they touch the soul." Animal communication, including man's, is "true, immediate," and speech is "in every sense" while sight "*speaks* to him." The effective wordplay on *scents* and *sense* enhances the poem's point that both cat's and man's senses quicken in "attentions and arousals in which an identity rearrives."

The fourth and fifth poems of book 1 and the fourth poem of book 2 clearly set forth the terms of order. "To Speak My Mind" (99–100) continues the motifs of "A Little Language," presenting the poet as a hunting hound, "predator of the marvelous." The colors of the spectrum, which had "articulate[d] / a promise" the cat remembered but could only imitate, returns as the poet, attending to the line, trying to sound it (in the dual senses of articulating it and plumbing its depths), trying to "divine the ratios" of sound and syllables, in effect serves to "keep alive / / in the sequence of vowels / / *l'arc-en-ciel marin* of the covenant." The song is a promise that follows "the flood / that comes to me" like Noah's rainbow after the deluge.

The ground of this poetry is faith in an order that is not man-made, as "Everything Speaks to Me" (100–02) asserts:

> Everything speaks to me!   In faith
> my sight is sound.   I draw from out
>   the resounding mountain side
> the gist of majesty.   It is at once
>   a presentation out of space
> awakening a spiritual enormity, and still,
>   the sounding of a tone
> apart from any commitment to some scale.

The poem's insistence that "words have weight in my hand / as I write. The argument / / is in the balance" is exemplified in these lines' insistence on the reader's awareness of the physical articulation of the high and low vowels, most evident in the repetitions of *sound, out, resounding, mountain,* and so forth, against the high vowel sounds of *speaks, faith, sight,* and so on. Quite "apart from any commitment to some scale" of insufferable grammarians, the lines truly bring home to the sympathetic reader their proposition that "In faith / my sight is sound."

The aptly titled "Our Art But to Articulate" (115–16), then, takes Dante's argument that Nature is God's art and extends it to mean, with Whitehead, that all our reality, including God, is in process, "In no thing final, in everything / / generate of finality." With large implications for his poetics, Duncan draws the string and lets fly: "even man's *miserere* / / among the animal variations belongs, / / expands the *Gloria* / / of the plan." Since "its law / / in all its sentences is true," since it must be what it is, there can be no mistakes.

Since such a proposition contrasts sharply with our anthropocentric view of, say, recent history, let us look at three consecutive poems derived from Dante's *De Monarchia* as well as from Olson's *Maximus.* "The Individual Man" (104–5) again cites Dante's lines about God's Art being Nature, and finds that while each man is unitary he is yet part of the whole, "having his nature and truth / outlined / in relation to groups" and seeking "harmonies in his / district / and in the city." Despite his contrasting title, "Of Empire" (105–6) presents another take on some of the very same lines, that the individual "finds / himself in freely attending, changing, / electing, or joining to carry forward / the idea, the insistent phrase, / the needed resonance into action." Finally, "The Meaning of Each Particular" (106–7) drives home the point, for both poetry and politics: we cannot know the whole, and so must concentrate on the immediate perception even as we recognize the need to live "beyond ourselves." As a key line reveals, "in the unit unity concentrated," even if "The sum is beyond us." No individual can realize the potential of the race. Duncan is not often credited for his humility.

With its puns on *atonality* and *atonement,* "The Household" (110–11) incorporates Dante's discussion of the canzone into Duncan's ideal for such resonance in the arrangement of the City. In turn, "Letting the Beat Go" (112–13) defends the set against charges of high-mindedness. In the face of contemporary cynicism, the poem insists that what "the mind beholds" is no less "real" for that. Why must mere materialism, and the sordid facts at that, be "all the real life here below": "the glutted cities, choked streams, / you think I do not know them all, / the 'facts' of this world. . . ? / They are the facts from which I fly / / aloft." The great poets, seen best in Shakespeare and Dante, do not leave the rest of us behind, according to "In Nothing Superior" (116–17). Rather, they present "a sublime community," never making their readers feel inferior but instead arousing their "whole capacity" to actualization. It is indeed ironic that Duncan's unfashionable eclecticism, which supports such large claims for poetry, is all too often turned against him by the very readers he would rouse to their fullest selves.

His poems, admittedly, make large demands on us, particularly his poems that confront us with our responsibilities. As Dante renounced Florence and prayed for her deliverance in his epistles to Henry VII, Duncan in the early 1970s renounced the United States, especially the Presidency and Congress, as in "Where the Fox of This Stench Sulks" (126–27)—"out of the people, out of the milling electorate, the millions at work at the / sick breasts of the Covenant, / / the hosts daily consuming their lives at the churning factories of war-goods and / stacks of commodities"—calling down an apocalypse of "just penalties"; as in "In Truth Doth She Breathe Out Poisonous Fumes" (128), with its pun on *news* and *noose*:

> I turn on the flow,
>   the flickering TV picture feed,

to watch the news,   the mind's noose
    of violence,   starved and assaulted bodies,
    of personality strut and show,
the mounting images of crisis,   the
strain that eats away at the nation.

So at last there is no escape. While the faith in the design remains
unshaken, the poet's conscience insists upon his individual responsibility to the community and to the language. An outrageous compar-
ison suggests itself: like the Calvinist who accepted his own sinfulness
in a world without free will, Duncan accepts his personal responsibility
in a world beyond his knowing. The final poem of book 3, "And a
Wisdom as Such" (131), with its own apt pun on *lets go* and *let's go*,
Duncan himself has called "a rapturous prayer for dissolution. . . . In
this longing for the close, the Me-Myself-and-I trinity is dissolved"
(FC 234). The poem is one more return to Olson's charge in "Against
Wisdom as Such" that Duncan invites the rushing-in of God, and Duncan accepts the charge in a "rapturous outpouring / speech of self" until
the self is emptied,

out from me, the very last of me,
till I am rid of every rind and seed
into that sweetness,
that final giving over, letting go,
that scattering of every nobleness . . . (Duncan's ellipses)

Few poets today, it hardly needs to be said, are willing to accept such
risks so totally. Whether or not one looks foolish, or loses one's audience, or finds one's self, is a matter for each reader to confront in this
poetry. It is certainly, at this point, a matter beyond literary criticism.

As nicely as the preceding paragraph would have ended this book,
Duncan's book will not be turned so easily to any aesthetic, political,
or literary critical purposes. *Ground Work* contains several more notable
lyrics, including "The Missionaries (Passages)" (135–36), a poem that
can be read as instructions for reading the "Passages" set and as a commentary on Duncan's withdrawal from a public role; and "The Torn
Cloth" (137–39), a poem that results from a mistake "not denied but
kept, / / as ever I spin out of kept feeling / / to let loose from my
keeping." The torn cloth, a metaphor for a rent friendship, generates
puns on *re-weaving* and *we-reaving,* but also on *bliss* and *blisterd,* and a

rime on the ripped "root-nerves / of my sciatic trunk-line," an allusion to Duncan's sciatica attack in 1975.

Finally, there is "An Interlude of Winter Light" (149–54). Even as I caught myself hoping I could omit this poem from my chapter so that it would "fit" my length limitations, this poem forced itself into this book. The poem demonstrates as it comments upon Duncan's poetic process, "as the river of fire in the poem comes / surpassing what the mind would *know*," incorporating puns (ours/hours, second-hour-first), multiple allusions, guesses, interruptions ("even as I dread it," the poet reports, at the Ballet Bejant "the old crone sitting next to me" barges into the poem, and later appears as "the curious insistent old woman, / ignorant Muse"), and mistakes. Persons the poet resists force their way into the poem and surprise him with unexpected gifts, as in Mallarmé: *"Je t'apporte le Don du poème."* In all this, he struggles—"(Let me get the record straight: / scene after scene is coming into this)"— and admits his deep confusion. "Misled we *must* be / or we would not have brought into the question / . . . / we would have forgotten . . . / . . . we would have known better / . . . / and we would never have come along this way." Not only do such generative strife and confusion look forward to the second volume of *Ground Work,* subtitled *In the Dark,* a phrase that appears in "An Interlude" as well as in many other poems of this first volume; they also serve as a warning and a lesson to his critics and readers: without such risks, losses, and confusion, "It would all / have been untroubled by that informing / duel of Night and the betraying blast / of the Day's light."

Notes and References

Preface

    1. Duncan to William Everson, "July 28 or So [1940]," *Sagetrieb* 4, no. 2/3 (1985):155.

Chapter One

    1. See the Tylers' memoir, "In the Beginning, or Recatching *The Years as Catches*," in *Robert Duncan: Scales of the Marvelous,* ed. Robert J. Bertholf and Ian W. Reid (New York: New Directions, 1979), 1–13.

    2. "The Homosexual in Society," *Politics* 1 (August 1944):209–11. This essay is reprinted by Ekbert Faas in his *Young Robert Duncan: Portrait of the Poet as Homosexual in Society* (Santa Barbara: Black Sparrow, 1983), 319–22. A revised and annotated version written in 1959 appears in *Jimmy & Lucy's House of "K"* 3 (1985):51–69.

    3. Duncan's preface to *One Night Stand & Other Poems* by Jack Spicer (San Francisco: Grey Fox, 1980):ix.

    4. Michael Davidson, "Disorders of the Net: The Poetry of Robert Duncan" (Ph.D. diss., SUNY Buffalo, 1971), 17.

    5. Charles Olson, "Against Wisdom As Such," *Black Mountain Review* 1 (1954):35–39; rpt. in *Human Universe and Other Essays* (New York: Grove, 1967).

Chapter Two

    1. Good discussions of Duncan's use of his derivations include Michael Davidson, "Cave of Resemblances, Cave of Rimes: Traditon and Repetition in Robert Duncan," *Ironwood* 22 (1983):33–45; Michael Andre Bernstein, "Bringing It All Back Home: Derivations and Quotations in Robert Duncan and the Poundian Tradition," *Sagetrieb* 1 (1982):176–89; and Bernstein, "Robert Duncan: Talent and the Individual Tradition," *Sagetrieb* 4, no. 2/3 (1985):177–90.

    2. On Duncan's Romantic ancestry, see Robert Bertholf, "Shelley, Stevens and Robert Duncan: The Poetry of Approximation," *Artful Thunder: Versions of the Romantic Tradition in American Literature in Honor of Howard P. Vincent,* ed. Robert DeMott and Sanford Marovitz (Kent: Kent State University Press, 1975), 269–99; Richard Haven, "Some Perspectives in Three Poems by Gray, Wordsworth, and Duncan," *Romantic and Modern: Revaluations of Literary Tradition,* ed. George Bornstein (Pittsburgh: University of Pittsburgh Press, 1977):69–88.

3. *The Works of Walt Whitman,* vol. 2. *The Collected Prose,* ed. Malcolm Cowley (New York: Minerva Press, 1969), 230.

4. *Coinherence,* a term borrowed from Charles Williams, names a key concept for Duncan, an experience of wholeness and immediacy related to what he elsewhere calls "a grace recognized by the writer in the reality of things" (FC 25). Duncan most directly describes such an experience in "Riding," from his book *Letters* (D 117–18).

5. Whitman, *Collected Prose,* 194.

6. Benjamin Lee Whorf, "Science and Linguistics," in his *Language, Thought, and Reality,* ed. John B. Carroll (New York: MIT Press and John Wiley & Sons, 1956), 213.

7. Whorf, "Language, Mind, and Reality," in *Language, Thought, and Reality,* 246–70.

8. Edward Sapir, *Language* (New York: Harcourt, Brace & Co., 1921), 244n, 242. See also *Selected Writings of Edward Sapir in Lanugage, Culture and Personality,* ed. David G. Mandelbaum (Berkeley: University of California Press, 1949).

9. William James, "A World of Pure Experience," in his *Essays in Radical Empiricism* (Cambridge: Harvard University Press, 1976), 35. *The Principles of Psychology,* 2 vols. (1890; rpt., New York: Dover, 1950).

10. A good discussion of Pound's influence on Duncan (as well as Olson's) is Don Byrd's "The Question of Wisdom as Such," *Scales of the Marvelous,* 38–55.

Chapter Three

1. Charles Olson, *The Maximus Poems,* ed. George Butterick (Berkeley: University of California Press, 1983), 249.

2. Barbara Herrnstein Smith, *Poetic Closure: A Study of How Poems End* (Chicago: University of Chicago Press, 1968), 2, 34, 175.

3. Alfred North Whitehead, *Process and Reality: An Essay in Cosmology* (1929; rpt., New York: The Free Press, 1969), 340. Subsequent references in this chapter cited as PR.

4. Heraclitus, *The Cosmic Fragments,* ed. G. S. Kirk (Cambridge: Cambridge University Press, 1970), 39. Wendy MacIntyre discusses the sources of Duncan's use of logos as "the generating Utterance" in "The Logos of Robert Duncan," *Maps* 6 (1974):81–98.

5. Robert Duncan in class, recorded 11 November 1977, Archive for New Poetry, University of California at San Diego, part 2, side 1.

6. Duncan said of "Passages," "All of them have closure as far as their quality as an individual poem. I love the closure and the individual part of a poem. I'm not carrying out a theory—there's nothing open about an individual 'Passage.' And so it's got interior composition. However, all of that is related to a thing that can't possibly have completion, so I can't not complete it. It's related throughout" (Ibid.).

7. Percy Bysshe Shelley, "A Defence of Poetry," *The Complete Works of Percy Bysshe Shelley,* ed. Roger Ingpen and Walter E. Peck (1926–1930; rpt., New York: Gordian Press, 1965), 124; see also Duncan, "Preface to a Reading of Passages 1–22," *Maps* 6 (1974): 53–55.

8. Gabriel Josipovici, *The Lessons of Modernism* (Totowa, NJ: Rowman and Littlefield, 1977), 138.

9. "Pages from a Notebook," *The Artist's View* 5 (July 1953):1.

10. Duncan to the author, 25 September 1978. See Siegfried Giedion, *Mechanization Takes Command* (New York: Oxford University Press, 1948), 477–78.

11. Smith, *Poetic Closure,* 233–34.

12. Duncan to the author, 25 September 1978.

Chapter Four

1. Hamilton and Mary Tyler, "In the Beginning," 5.

2. For a radically different view that "the Forties constitutes his greatest period," see William Everson, "Of Robert Duncan," *Credences* 8/9 (1980):147–51.

3. Duncan to Jonathan Williams, undated. Poetry/Rare Books Collection, the University Libraries, SUNY Buffalo. Robert J. Bertholf and Ruth Nurmi provide a different but not mutually exclusive reading of *The Venice Poem* in "'Scales of the Marvelous': Robert Duncan's 'the Venice Poem,'" *New Poetry* 23, no. 2 (1976):22–32.

4. See Jane Harrison, *Epilegomena and Themis* (1912, 1921; rpt., New Hyde Park, NY: University Books, 1962), 31, 45.

5. See. M. L. Rosenthal, *The New Poets* (New York: Oxford University Press, 1967), 174–84.

6. *The Artist's View* 5 (July 1953):2.

7. Gertrude Stein, *The Autobiography of Alice B. Toklas* (1933), in *Selected Writings,* ed. Carl Van Vechten (New York: Modern Library, 1962), 194.

8. Duncan to Jonathan Williams, 19 November 1956. Poetry/Rare Books Collection, The University Libraries, SUNY Buffalo.

Chapter Five

1. Michael Davidson, "A Book of First Things: *The Opening of the Field,*" in *Scales of the Marvelous,* 56–84, provides a good sense of the book as a whole, and pp. 66–67 deal specifically with "The Structure of Rime."

Chapter Six

1. Thomas Carlyle, "The Hero As Poet: Dante; Shakespeare," in *On Heroes, Hero-Worship and the Heroic in History* (1841; rpt. New York: Scribner's, 1901), 101. Page references immediately following quotations appear in text.

2. Duncan's poem, "Source," from *Letters* (D 130) throws additional light on his recasting of the Arethusa story.

3. Denise Levertov, "Claritas," *O Taste and See* (New York: New Directions, 1964), 35–36.

4. George Quasha, "Duncan Reading," *Credences* 8/9 (1980):170.

Chaper Seven

1. Joseph Frank, "Spatial Form in Modern Literature," in *The Widening Gyre* (Bloomington: Indiana University Press, 1963), 3–62. The following two paragraphs draw heavily on a conversation with Michael Davidson; see also his essay, "A Book of First Things" cited above, as well as Duncan's "Notes on the Structure of Rime" and "Preface to a Reading of Passages 1-22," both in *Maps* 6 (1974):42–55.

2. Ian W. Reid, "The Plural Text: 'Passages,'" in *Scales of the Marvelous*, 162.

3. Robert Duncan, "Ideas of the Meaning of Form," three lectures at the 1973 National Poetry Festival, Thomas Jefferson College, Allendale, MI; Master Tape #470; subsequent references in this chapter cited as NPF.

4. Whitehead, *Process and Reality*, 83; subsequent references in this chapter cited as PR.

5. These principles are discussed in most basic physics books, such as Robert K. Adair's *Concepts in Physics* (New York: Academic Press, 1969). I have also consulted Isaac Asimov, *Understanding Physics*, vol. 3 (New York: Walker and Co., 1966), and Wolfgang Pauli, *Pauli Lectures on Physics: Volume 1. Electrodynamics* (Cambridge: MIT Press, 1973).

6. Brian Hayes, "The Heart of Matter," *New Republic*, 4 July 1983, 37–38.

7. Robert C. Weber, "Robert Duncan and the Poem of Resonance," *Concerning Poetry* 11, 1 (1978):70. I have tried to avoid duplicating this intelligent reading of "The Fire."

8. Venturi, *The 16th Century from Leonardo to El Greco* (New York: Skira, 1956), 33–35.

9. This influential essay first appeared in *Poetry New York* 3 (1950) and is reprinted in *Human Universe*.

10. "A Note on Tone in Poetry," *Literary Behavior: Writers' Conference Report*, a mimeographed publication of the students' Writers' Conference at UC Berkeley, fall semester, 1948–49, 53–54. Cited by Faas, *Young Robert Duncan*, 260.

Chapter Eight

1. Duncan to Jonathan Williams, 11 December 1971, Poetry/Rare Books Collection, The University Libraries, SUNY Buffalo.

2. Mark Rudman, "The Right Chaos, the Right Vagueness," *New York*

Times Book Review, 4 August 1985: 13–14; Helen Vendler, ed. *The Harvard Book of Contemporary American Poetry* (Cambridge: The Belknap Press, 1985); M. L. Rosenthal and Sally M. Gall, *The Modern Poetic Sequence: The Genius of Modern Poetry* (New York: Oxford University Press, 1983).

3. For the fullest statement of Duncan's frustrations with publishers, see his preface to *Maps* 6 (1974):1–16.

4. Andrew Schelling, "Of Maps, Castelli, Warplanes, & Divers Other Things That Come 'Before the War,'" *Jimmy & Lucy's House of "K"* 3 (1985), 44.

5. Ronald Johnson, "The Fertile Ground," *Jimmy & Lucy's House of "K"* 3 (1985), 31–32, and Schelling, "Of Maps," 48–51.

6. Michael Davidson, "A Felt Architectonics of the Numinous: Robert Duncan's *Ground Work,*" *Sulfur* 12 (1985):135.

7. Thomas Parkinson, "Robert Duncan's *Ground Work,*" *Southern Review* 21 (1985):60.

8. Jed Rasula, "The American Poetry Wax Museum," *Jimmy & Lucy's House of "K"* 3 (1985), 70–71.

9. Levertov, *To Stay Alive* (New York: New Directions, 1972); see her "Memoir and a Critical Tribute" in *Scales of the Marvelous,* 85–115, where she continues to insist that "Duncan's affectionate anxiety" for her was "in a sense misplaced."

10. Thom Gunn, *Moly and My Sad Captains* (New York: Farrar, Straus and Giroux, 1973), 5–7; hereafter cited as Gunn.

11. Recorded on a tape in the Archive for New Poetry, University of California at San Diego.

Selected Bibliography

PRIMARY SOURCES

1. Poetry

Audit 4, 1 (1967). A special Duncan issue.

Bending the Bow. New York: New Directions, 1968; rpt., London: Fulcrum Press, 1971.

A Book of Resemblances: Poems 1950–1953. New Haven: Henry Wenning, 1966.

Caesar's Gate: Poems 1949–1950 with Collages by Jess Collins. Palma de Mallorca: Divers Press, 1955; rpt. as *Caesar's Gate: Poems 1949–1950 with Paste-ups by Jess.* Berkeley: Sand Dollar, 1972.

Derivations: Selected Poems 1950–1956. London: Fulcrum Press, 1968.

The First Decade: Selected Poems 1940–1950. London: Fulcrum Press, 1968.

The Five Songs. San Diego: Friends of the UCSD Library, 1981.

Fragments of a Disorderd Devotion. San Francisco: privately printed, 1952; rpt., San Francisco: Gnomon Press, and Toronto: Island Press, 1966.

Ground Work: Before the War. New York: New Directions, 1984.

Heavenly City, Earthly City. Berkeley: Bern Porter, 1947.

Letters: Poems MCMLIII–MCMLVI. Highlands, NJ: Jargon, 1958.

Medieval Scenes. San Francisco: Centaur Press, 1950; rpt. as *Medieval Scenes 1950 and 1959* with a preface by Duncan and an afterword by Robert J. Bertholf. Kent: The Kent State University Libraries, 1978.

An Ode and Arcadia (with Jack Spicer). Berkeley: Ark, 1974.

The Opening of the Field. New York: Grove, 1960; rpt., London: Jonathan Cape, 1969, and New York: New Directions, 1973.

Passages 22–27: Of the War. Berkeley: Oyez, 1966.

Play Time Pseudo Stein. New York: The Poet's Press, 1969; rpt., San Francisco: The Tenth Muse, 1969.

Poems 1948–49. Berkeley: Berkeley Miscellany Editions, 1949.

Poetic Disturbances. Berkeley: May Quarto, 1970.

Roots and Branches. New York: Scribners, 1964; rpt., New York: New Directions, 1968, and London: Jonathan Cape, 1970.

Selected Poems. San Francisco: City Lights Books, 1959.

Six Prose Pieces. Mt. Horeb, WI: Perishable Press, 1966.

Tribunals: Passages 31–35. Los Angeles: Black Sparrow, 1970.

Veil, Turbine, Cord & Bird. Brooklyn: Jordan Davies, 1979.

The Venice Poem. Sidney, Australia: Prism, 1975.

Writing Writing a Composition Book: Stein Imitations. Albuquerque, NM: Sumbooks, 1964.
The Years as Catches: First Poems (1939–1946). Berkeley: Oyez, 1966.

2. Prose and Drawings
As Testimony: The Poem & the Scene. San Francisco: White Rabbit Press, 1964.
The Cat and the Blackbird. San Francisco: White Rabbit Press, 1967. (Children's book).
Fictive Certainties. New York: New Directions, 1985.
A Selection of 65 Drawings from One Drawing-Book 1952–1956. Los Angeles: Black Sparrow, 1970.
The Truth & Life of Myth: An Essay in Essential Autobiography. New York: House of Books, Ltd., 1968; rpt., Fremont, MI: The Sumac Press (in cooperation with SOMA Books), 1973.

3. Uncollected Essays and Articles.
"As Testimony: Reading Zukofsky These Forty Years." *Paideuma* 7, 3 (1978): 421–27.
"Crisis of Spirit in the Word." *Credences* n.s. 2, 1 (1982): 63–68. (Sermon.)

"The H. D. Book"
Part I: *Beginnings*
Chapter 1: *Coyote's Journal* 5/6 (1966): 8–31.
Chapter 2: *Coyote's Journal* 8 (1967): 27–35.
Chapter 3: *Tri-Quarterly* 12 (Spring 1968): 67–82.
Chapter 4: *Tri-Quarterly* 12 (Spring 1968): 82–98.
Chapter 5: "Occult Matters," *Stony Brook* 1/2 (Fall 1968): 4–19.
Chapter 6: "Rites of Participation, Part I," *Caterpillar* 1 (October 1967): 6–29.
Chapter 6: "Rites of Participation, Part II," *Caterpillar* 2 (January 1968): 125–54.
Part Two: *Nights and Days*
"From the Day Book—excerpts from an extended study of H. D.'s poetry." *Origin* 10, second series (July 1963):1–47.
Chapter 1: *Sumac* 1, 1 (Fall 1968):101–46.
Chapter 2: *Caterpillar* 6 (January 1969):16–38.
Chapter 3: *Io* 6 (Summer 1969):117–40.
Chapter 4: *Caterpillar* 7 (April 1969):27–60.
Chapter 5: section one, *Stony Brook* 3/4 (Fall 1969):336–47. section two, *Credences* 2 (August 1975):50–52. This material is repeated with minor changes and with additional sections of Chapter 5 in *Sagetrieb* 4, 2/3 (1985):39–86.
Chapter 6: *Southern Review* 21, 1 (January 1985): 26–48.

Chapter 7: *Credences* 2 (August 1975):53–67.
Chapter 8: *Credences* 2 (August 1975):68–94.
Chapter 9: *Chicago Review* 30, 3 (Winter 1979):37–88.
Chapter 10: *Ironwood* 22 (1983):48–65.
Chapter 11: *Montemora* 8 (1981):79–113.

"The Homosexual in Society." *Politics* 1 (1944):209–11.
"Iconographical Extensions," introduction to catalogue of *Translations by Jess*.
New York: Odyssia Gallery, 1971; also printed in a limited edition by
Black Sparrow.
"Notes on Grossinger's *Solar Journal.*" Santa Barbara: *Black Sparrow, n.d., n.p.*

4. Drama
Faust Foutu: An Entertainment in Four Parts. Stinson Beach, CA: Enkidu Sur-
rogate, 1959.
Medea at Kolchis: The Maiden Head. Berkeley: Oyez, 1965.

5. Interviews
Abbott, Steve and Aaron Shurin. "Interview/Workshop with Robert Duncan."
Soup 1 (1980):30–57, 79.
Abbott and Shurin. "Interview: Robert Duncan." *Gay Sunshine* 40/41
(1979):1–8.
Balzano, Carol. "Poet Robert Duncan: Out from Under 'Olson's Push.'" *Prod-
igal Son* 1, no. 17 (12–19 February 1982): 1–3; continued, "Revolt
Against 'Backlash.'" *Prodigal Son* 1, no. 18 (20–26 February 1982):4–5.
Bernstein, Michael Andre, and Burton Hatlen. "Interview with Robert Dun-
can." *Sagetrieb* 4, 2/3 (1985):87–135.
Bowering, George, and Robert Hogg. *Robert Duncan: An Interview, April 19,
1969.* A Beaver Kosmos Folio. Toronto: The Coach House Press, 1971.
Callahan, Bob. "The World of Jaime de Angulo." *Netzahualcoyotl News* 1, 1
(1979):1–5, 14–16.
Cohn, Jack R., and Thomas J. O'Donnell. "An Interview with Robert Dun-
can." *Contemporary Literature* 21 (1984):513–48.
Cohn and O'Donnell. "'The Poetry of Unevenness': An Interview with Robert
Duncan." *Credences* n.s. 3, 2 (1985):91–111.
Faas, Ekbert. "Interview: Robert Duncan." *Towards a New American Poetics:
Essays & Interviews.* Ed. Ekbert Faas. Santa Barbara: Black Sparrow, 1978.
Gluck, Robert. "Robert Duncan: A Vast, Nervous, Contradictory, Worldly
Life." *Advocate* 397 (26 June 1984):35–40.
Hamalian, Linda. "Robert Duncan on Kenneth Rexroth." *Conjunctions* 4
(1983):85–95.
Kamenetz, Rodger. "Realms of Being: An Interview with Robert Duncan."
Southern Review 21, 1 (1985):5–25.

Mesch, Howard. "Robert Duncan's Interview." *Unmuzzled Ox* 4, no. 2 (1977):79–96.

Nicosia, Gerald. "'The Closeness of Mind': An Interview with Robert Duncan." *Unspeakable Visions of the Individual* 12 (1981):13–27.

"Reflector Interview: Robert Duncan." *Reflector,* student magazine at Shippensburg (PA) State University (1982): 49–59.

Vance, Eugene, and David Schaff. "On Poetry." *Yale Reports* 328 (31 May 1964);1–9.

SECONDARY SOURCES

1. Bibliography

Bertholf, Robert. *Robert Duncan: A Descriptive Bibliography.* Santa Rosa: Black Sparrow, 1986.

2. Books and Special Issues of Magazines

Bertholf, Robert J., and Ian W. Reid, eds. *Robert Duncan: Scales of the Marvelous.* New York: New Directions, 1979. Essays and tributes by various hands, including those cited above by Hamilton and Mary Tyler, Don Byrd, Michael Davidson, Denise Levertov, and Ian Reid, as well as Eric Mottram's "Heroic Survival Through Ecstatic Form: Robert Duncan's *Roots and Branches,"* Thom Gunn's "Homosexuality in Robert Duncan's Poetry," Nathaniel Mackey's "Uroboros: *Dante* and *A Seventeenth Century Suite,"* and others.

Faas, Ekbert. *Young Robert Duncan: Portrait of the Poet as Homosexual in Society.* Santa Barbara: Black Sparrow, 1983. Despite some errors of fact and tone, a very detailed biography through 1950.

Ironwood 22 (1983). Work by and about Duncan. Especially good are Michael Davidson's essay on Duncan's eclectic literary genealogy cited above, as well as Wendy MacIntyre's "Psyche, Christ and the Poem" with its good close reading of "Epilogos," and Charles Molesworth's "Truth and Life and Robert Duncan" on the role of the spiritual in Duncan's poetry and on his use of metaphor.

Maps 6 (1974). Work by and about Duncan.

Sagetrieb 4, 2/3 (1985). Essays, poems and memoirs, including Bernstein's cited above, Joseph G. Kronick's "Robert Duncan and the Truth That Lies in Myth," R. S. Hamilton's "After Strange Gods: Robert Duncan Reading Ezra Pound and H. D.," and others.

3. Articles and Parts of Books.

Bertholf, Robert J. "Shelley, Stevens, and Robert Duncan: The Poetry of Approximations." *Artful Thunder: Versions of the Romantic Tradition in*

American Literature in Honor of Howard P. Vincent. Ed. Robert J. DeMott
and Sanford E. Marovitz. Kent: Kent State University Press, 1975.
Places Duncan clearly in the Romantic tradition of process and open
form.

Bromige, David. "Beyond Prediction." *Credences* 2 (1975):101–13. A personal essay in response to Duncan's "Moving the Moving Image" that
frankly confronts and engages the difficulty of reading an open-ended
poem in full awareness that consciousness is "more strobe than spotlight."

Mackey, Nathaniel. "The World-Poem in Microcosm: Robert Duncan's 'The
Continent.'" *ELH* 47 (1980):595–618. Not only an informative reading
of the title poem, but an effective lesson in how to read Duncan's work.

Mersmann, James F. *Out of the Vietnam Vortex: A Study of Poets and Poetry
Against the War.* Lawrence: University Press of Kansas, 1974, 159–204.
Analyzes Duncan's poetics, biography, and cosmology, showing how
their joint concern for both community and individual volition inform
Duncan's reaction to the war.

Michelson, Peter. "A Materialist Critique of Robert Duncan's Grand Collage." *Boundary* 8, 2 (1980): 21–43. A provocative, careful reading of
Duncan's work, and a thoughtful attack on his idealist aesthetics as "a
profound ethical agnosticism."

Nelson, Cary. *Our Last First Poets: Vision and History in Contemporary American
Poetry.* Urbana: University of Illinois Press, 1981, 97–144. Despite an
unfortunate warp caused by Nelson's political and literary biases, a
thoughtful and probing reading of Duncan's poetics and of several poems,
with a focus on the effects of current historical events on the poetry.

Paul, Sherman. *The Lost America of Love: Rereading Robert Creeley, Edward
Dorn, and Robert Duncan.* Baton Rouge: LSU Press, 1981, 169–276. A
"reading diary," accepting the poets' terms that discursive language is the
enemy. Less a critical study of the poets than a dialogue with them,
valuable both for Paul's insightful responses and his exemplary openness
to the poems.

Quasha, George. "Duncan Reading." *Credences* 8/9 (1980): 162–75. Discusses Duncan's "reflexive reading" between text and poet and between
both of these and the reader, and demonstrates convincingly that there is
no "right way" to read Duncan except to explore "the Happening of the
text."

Thurley, Geoffrey. *The American Moment: American Poetry in the Mid-Century.*
New York: St. Martin's Press, 1977, 139–155. An example of how not
to read Duncan. His chapter on Duncan typifies the negative reaction to
Duncan's work by critics who attack him for doing exactly what he is
trying to do, e.g., complaining about poems "which fail to become
poems (properly speaking) and slide into one another"; who dislike his
"general inner softness, a certain lack of intellectual and moral rigour";
or who otherwise reveal a greater need for elucidation than for poetry.

Index